THE
VIEW
FROM DELPHI

Rhapsodies of Hellenic Wisdom

and

An Ecstatic Appreciation of Western History

Frank Marrero

ΕΝΕΛΥΣΙΟΣ

Sybil
Tripod
Spirit

This book is dedicated to

Avatara Adi Da Samraj,

Eleutherios, the Liberator,

Whom I am graced to call Beloved.

An Apology for "Rhapsody"

Orpheus sang and taught about "divine realization" in "flowing sutras", *rhapsodos,* often translated as "song stitches". "Rhapsody" can be characterized as the theological weaving between sacred poesy and prosaic philosophy.

This text seeks to both illuminate that Orphic rhapsody and emulate it. Herein you will find a logical picture that is idealistically painted with academic colors and strokes of both legend and report. Such blessing exaggeration is needed to sufficiently suggest that beauteous mystery which is beyond knowing.

Table of Contents

Preface and Acknowledgements: The Trail of Eleutherios

Three gods in the ancient Hellenic pantheon— Zeus, Dionysus, and Eros—held the esoteric surname *Eleutherios,* meaning "the Liberator" (root *eleuthera,* "free"). *Zeus Eleutherios* (*Zeus:* "Bright-Day"— Sanskrit *dyas*, "bright") was the keeper of liberty, armies of liberation knew his lightning bolts would be their ally, within and without. Mystics spoke of the liberation of Zeus as the inextinguishable brightness beyond the underworld. *Dionysus Eleutherios* bequeathed his favor through free feeling, celebration, and ecstasy. *Eros Eleutherios* shot his arrows through the heart and the liberation of love was given. At last, Love married the once arrogant and mistrusting princess Psyche before Zeus Himself, whose ambrosia gave her immortality. These gods of brightness, ecstasy, and love each describe the divinity which grants freedom.

The great goddess Hera also held the name *Eilythea*, said to be derived from Eleutherios, for the liberating divinity felt in childbirth. A new life is liberated from the womb. Springs near temples often carried the appellation *Eilythea*—for their purest waters were used in childbirth.

Twenty-seven centuries ago, five generations *before* the "golden age" was to begin, there was an "Orphic-cleanser and initiator" named Epimenides, the most spiritual of the Seven Sages, who was known to carry the epithet *Eleutherios.* Though little history was kept, it was particularly noted that Epimenides, "greatest master of all the magically gifted men" came at the behest of the Oracle of Delphi to a "plagued-filled" Athens on the verge of civil war between the aristocracy and the people of the villages. It was trumpted how his company held sacred power and he engaged in "potent religious ceremonies of which his wisdom alone knew the secrets."

Working with the poet and statesman Solon, who had petitioned the Oracle, Epimenides spoke to the populace, conducted public rituals, and gave Athens new laws, to cleanse it from its impurities. It was reported that the ecstasy of his religious power *liberated* the city from "the polluting spirit," and the laws then held the new purity.

Epimenides, the Initiator and Liberator, hailed from *Eleuthernai*, "ancient Orphic centre of Kathartic wisdom," near the cave of Zeus on Mt. Ida above the Minoan expanse. Religious lore tells us of his Orphic mastery and purity: his prolonged fasting, his worship of the "underworld Zeus," his "god-possessed wisdom," his divine ignorance, and the vibrant *transmission* of divine communion via the "long ecstasy of his soul." His demonstration of "constant ecstasy" enabled anyone to feel and thus recognize the liberation rendered by communion and divine company.

And upon the behest of the Oracle at Delphi, the Athenians built temple *Eleutherios* upon the great plains of Platea, commemorating the greatest of all Greek victories for their freedom.

And below Dionysus' statue in Athens, sanctifying the birthplace of theatre, the name

"Dionysus" was not carved below his feet; only the highest Orphic epithet for the raving god of theatre: *Eleutherios*.

In November 2008, a divine-man passed from this life (into *Mahasamadhi* or *The Great Ecstasy*) who called himself by the ancient mystic name *Eleutherios*. I sought, came upon, and enjoyed the extraordinary companionship and instruction of Avatara Adi Da, Samraj, Eleutherios (lit: The Descended One in Person, Original Giver, Royal World-Teacher, Liberator) for over three decades.

I was hearkened back again and again to an ancient time as the calm brilliance and mysterious vibrancy of his giving company initiated in me a graceful process of self-understanding and sacred submission. Via the power of his initiatory and baptismal influence washing us in sheer joy and prior consciousness, I have learned the practice of purifying self-observation "in the face of" Heart-imbued Presence. In the mysterious silence of his mere company, I have come to fundamental and divine Ignorance, emptied in mindless wonder and undone in the mindful awe of inherent radiance. Because of his Touch, I learned to give my self to divine possession and the blissful paradox of supreme being.

Like in Orphic times, I learned about the internal, subtle anatomy of human potentiality through direct initiation and divine transmission from a Liberator. Like in Orphic times, mystery exceeded knowledge, and I was led beyond the mind to the Source Condition of the mind, the world, and the blissful body.

Enlightened by the vibrant radiance of this free standing man, I then investigated the mystical origins of the pre-Socratic Mystery schools, using the word "Eleutherios" as a guide. I followed the tree of the mystic wisdom I encountered and what I found is presented here—and in ancient Orphic style—in speech that is more mused than surmised; a rhapsodic song of recollections and revelations.

Let me be very clear about the "academic" nature of these writings. I have read the research and much of the original texts and I choose my words in grounded academics. However, my organization and representation is not "academic" in the usual mental way, a collection of "facts" and postulates in a conventional scholarly presentation. Rather, my renderings of the ancient wisdom are heartily informed by the initiations of spiritual baptisms given to me by Adi Da Eleutherios. This spiritual influence allows me to read the research differently than the usual heady academics or even the splendorous romantic aesthetics. Indeed, after examining the findings, I proceeded as a forensic artist, reconstructing the religious face of our ancestors with both poetic and realistic complexion.

There is ancient precedent for this rhapsodic freedom in academic arenas. Indeed, the word "academy" comes from Akademus, the hero of a heritage family that would lead to Plato and his Academy. On the road to Eleusis, about six stadia from the Double Gates, amidst an extensive cathedral of heritage plana trees and olive orchards, tended flower gardens, and the babbling waters of a small river, *academic* language was originally closer to a rhapsodic *gnosis* than the collection of provable facts. There, I take my stand once more, speaking outside the city gates, again surrounded by groves, brooks, and divinities, freed of mere mentality by holy mysteries.

The ancient Hellenes noticed that a sound that is too repetitive would soon not be noticed. That which is closest to us is quickly lost in familiarity, they observed. As a Westerner, I am moved to share a sacred inheritance that is hardly recognized by us, invisible in its closeness. The spiritual origin of logical thinking is often overlooked, or negated by the immature, merely logical mind.

The divine knowledge which inspired the West is exalting and liberating like many of the other ways of knowing in the Great Tradition of humanity's wisdom, but with the added advantage that it is already encoded in Western psyches and in the form of our culture— eminently recognizable and spiritually usable as we re-discover and remember our original religious truth.

Fools are those, Heraklitos exclaimed, that are not in constant intercourse with their own nature. Westerners need not look only to the East for high spiritual issues. The ancients of the West have left Westerners a legacy of truths in dearest terms—one that transmits Being and Truth, the Free and Formless Self-Existing Bright One — the Divine Reality Itself: Coincident with the infinity of forms which make up the Kosmos.

This mysterious awareness and understanding beyond myth and mentality which seems to possess us in times of grace and openness grounds the heart-glory *and* logical foundation of our Hellenic legacy. "True philosphy begins in wonder," proclaimed Sage Sokrates.

Our ancestors, East and West, opened their feeling and minds and followed the spirit of the body in ascending harmonies to subtleties of undying nectars as the body, mind, and feeling-intuition became resonant in a pure or erotic unity—and the tongue was set free in this raving joy.

Mentality was observed to be the lowest of the "subtle elements," even as it logically points to spectral dimensions of growth -- where each succeeding dimension holographically integrates and mystically envelops previous levels of adaptation, all the while leading to *and* enjoying the joyous origin of all thoughts and things.

Such stillness, equanimity, and harmony is the preparation for Orphic "self-realization", the "years of pleasure", and "eternal celebration". Discovering the roots of my own spiritual tradition in the West inspired me to share this ancient *philosophia,* blossoming *physis* and divine *theologoia* with you.

In the manner of the ancients, I heartily acknowledge the fair-voiced Kalliope who sang me epics, and Klio, the Muse of History, for her sweet visitations. Alas, my telling carries a limitation, a point of view, as all tellings must. From another view, another truth may be trumpeted, but this telling is lost in Delphi. I have stood upon the Temple and I utter these rhapsodies from there. I have laid my hands upon the stone that is transparent to time.

Forwith, I do not speak with the authority of a scholar, recounting with exactitude and concluding with certainty, but rather as one who attends a sacred fire, sharing a wonder across centuries.

Accordingly, I cannot extend enough praise to Adi Da Eleutherios, so great were his free gifts to me. I ask you to envision love so intimate — even from afar — that thoughts and breath are shared; so dear that one is naturally un-done in the nectar of love's perfect embrace. For hours upon end, inviting endlessness, Adi Da's Company washed and engulfed me in such depth of Heart-Joy and Bright Consciousness that "bliss" is too weak a description.

While the Master of the Mysteries instructed me, inspired me, tested and empowered me, more than anything that I recall from his company is an unbridled love. Like the love of my family, he held me and every single one absolutely dear. And he set fire to everything that I unknowingly put before the Heart Itself. There has been no other gift in my life, no summary of all other experiences and knowledge that compares to the unfathomable divinity of his loving company.

Because of the glory of my master, an understanding of human development and history dawned upon me. I came to understand my body's inheritance and, as a Westerner, fell in love with Delphi.

I was privileged to write in the Temple at Delphi.

Introduction: The Forms of Delphi

Language is, first of all, the interruption of silence. Mysteriously, we intuit how every word, even the most factual or concrete, is fundamentally poetic, hearkening to the silent point of understanding.

Language is, in every tongue and text, only a thread of what is communicated. Tones and postures, depth and context are also tacitly woven in wide textures.

Language is, like every other growing body, a living, breathing process—and words (every one and all) are vibrantly alive, each echoing a long lineage of sound and reflection. This aural inheritance can be heard in sentence, song, and verse, as we reach back to a distant time of simpler sounds and simpler meanings.

Speech may suddenly loom symphonic as a dance of form and feeling—even carry one away into a time of musing and ancient understanding. While a few words in our language have come to us essentially unchanged through millennia, most words are the product of seasoned transformation and growth—and all word-sounds communicate, even if unbeknownst to our verbal mind, their deep roots in silent ground.

"Delphi" is an ancient word in line with *delph*, or "hollow," and *delphys*, meaning "womb." In turn, del- conveys "manifesting" and phy- connotes light. The womb manifests light. To give light is to give birth—through an open, hollow place. Delphi poetically describes the religious nature of man and woman.

From this bright fertility, a new understanding and a new age of wisdom was born — which became "Western" civilization. To the degree that the Hellenes were the foundation of Western culture, Delphi was its pronounced womb and spiritual center. If we want to understand the Hellenic foundations which defined Western civilization — indeed if we want to understand ourselves — we must understand her womb, Delphi.

A child changes dramatically from infancy to adulthood, and yet there is a distinctive thread which remains the same even amidst the changes. The child is in the adult just as the adult is in the child. In the same way, Western civilization has both dramatically changed and remained distinctively the same. This rational and logical insistence begat *philosophia, schools, musiki, physics, mathematics, harmony, poetry, theatre, rhapsodies, katharis, theology, athletics, skepticism, therapy, history, democracy, logos, kosmos* ... in short, the culture, mind, and understanding into which all Westerners were born.

The Illiad and *The Odyssey*, Homer's foundational words for all Hellenes, turn upon the Trojan horse of Odysseus. The nine year war was at a stalemate. Odysseus strategically proposed using the Trojans' own symbolic animal, the horse, to leverage their mythic-mindedness. Calculating Odysseus became archetype for the advantage that cunning gives over mythic-literalism. But while the more cunning ones achieved victory, wily Odysseus had one hell of time getting home, revealing the disadvantage that guile also carries.

From the mythic metaphor of the Trojan horse grew the capacity of what would become known as *logos*. Upon Homer's *Illiad* and *Odysessy*, Orpheus then taught that there were two ways to comprehend the myths: the *demotiki,* or "vulgar" people, took them more literally while the sophisticated appreciated the myths to be *ouranos*, conveying a heavenly and allegorical meaning, where the surface story has logical implications. Indeed, Orpheus was known as the first *theologoi*, or "theologian".

Two centuries later, in the early morning of this myth-shattering understanding in the West, Anaxagoras proclaimed, "The sun is not a god, but a fiery rock, and it's probably larger than the Peloponnese." He was, you might have guessed, convicted of impiety to the god Helios, and forced to leave Athens to escape the drink of hemlock.

Our logical passage beyond mythic intelligence is not just a historical, cultural moment: it is a process each of us must go through in order to mature. *To understand that which had been believed is the beginning of ordinary human maturation* and true social and religious tolerance. This vaulting of logos beyond mythos describes both Western civilization and a sobriety in each of us.

The story of this leap in the West was said to be born from Delphi, where we may again take a stand, and from this foundation appreciate the changing drama as well as the distinctive sameness. To fully appreciate ourselves anew, let us look first at the "womb" from which *logos* and Westerners were born, and then view the growing child that became Western civilization.

Let it be observed: to understand history, it is necessary to understand the spectrum of human potentiality. Patterns of history can be compared insightfully to the unfoldment of a single individual. Without an inspiring and nuanced, full-spectrum and penetrating vision of human growth, history and maturation are misrepresented, however factual they may pretend to be.

History is not cyclic, as some postulate, except that, like individuals, history goes through cycles in its growth process. Cultures, people and epochs have their spiralling ups and downs, always growing and surging forward (while as a whole falling back not quite as far). However slowly our growth is proceeding, history mirrors the spectrum of human potentiality, falls back, and grows again—just like everyone, every time, every culture. There is a greater person, an oversoul if you will, emerging in every culture, including the new global matrix, growing up like any single person; this is her story, history.

The view from Delphi, like her growing child of Western civilization, vaults upwards in kaleidoscopic brilliance. Poised high on a terrace in a hollow, half-way up the mountain of Parnassos, there is the breathtaking beauty of the Sanctuary, overlooking the sea of olive orchards below --- the magnificent cliffs (the "Shining Ones") looming dominantly above and around you, the Temple of Apollo standing luminescently upon the scalloped terrace, and the gushing of the waters of the sacred spring Kastalia—where grateful pilgrims have quenched their thirst for millennia.

It is said that a thousand cities, "dotting the Mediterranean pond like frogs," began with fire carried by pilgrims from the Delphic hearth and the blessing of the Oracle upon their hearts. At a pivotal time in history, Delphi was the most adorned place on Earth, with all the Mediterranean world gifting it with art and wealth. This sacred ground served as the common hearth and cultural birthplace for all Hellenes and dessiminated their central calendar. The Hellenes honored Delphi as spiritual source, womb, and "our national divinity," explicitly.

How the Sanctuary must have looked walking up the Sacred Way during a celebration! Imagine the holiest of grounds, with thousands of statues or immortal personages; with its treasuries and holy places along the Way, and all the art and statuary adorned in new paints or fresh oils to glisten in the sunlight; with art of gold and jewels and masterfully

made gifts, the Way lined with praising pilgrims, and all coming in overwhelming waves of delight until at last one beheld the Temple itself, the Heart of this world, seat of the Oracle and the timeless Omphallos. The experience of Delphi must have been extreme, overwhelming, fully absorbing, blessing every pilgrim with beauty's awe.

To fully understand the sacred nature of Delphi, it is necessary to review the mythological and historical accounts of this holy ground. Then we will be prepared to fully comprehend the Orphic-imbued logos and spirit — the metaphysical, meta-magical, meta-mythic, and meta-ordinary communication. That communication is not confined to childish religious belief nor philosophical abstraction, but is found in *ek-stasis*, the favor of the gods.

The uniqueness of Delphi was not just in poetic meaning, nor confined to its mythical aura, or even its religious and political power. Combine Delphi's famous oracular prophecies with its sixteen centuries as "the center of the world," and mysteriously Delphi becomes a place that holds a certain transparency to time itself. Famous and revered prophecies — messages transparent to time — were ceremoniously and regularly issued by the Sibyl beside the Still Omphallos and Sacred Fire in the Temple of Apollo. And just as the child and the adult are reflected in each other, Westerners can look back upon our infancy at Delphi with a certain timeless transparency. *The View from Delphi* is the eyes looking back and to here.

From the healing temple at Epidavros to the Mysteries of divine initiation at Eleusis, from the elegance of Delos to the crucible of Athena's great city, from the prophecies at Delphi to the reverence for the world-wonder Zeus at his Temple at Olympia, our Western forefathers and foremothers ritually and ceremoniously brought the sacred revelation of divine ecstasy to their cultural family. Mythos vaulted to logos twenty-seven centuries ago as ecstasy transported story to a theological understanding that spiritually integrated body, emotion, mind, being, and world.

Ecstasy—from *ek-stasis*, "to stand out (from oneself)" — stands not only out of self and mind, but, because it speaks of "immortal happiness," stands also out of time. Stepping beyond the merely mortal vision, another view from Delphi unravels before us. It is an ecstatic appreciation of history. We are freed from the past in ecstasy, and a time-free appreciation of history allows us to more properly locate ourselves in the glorious presence. The cultural forms which were our foundation and reference are outgrown in a balanced, unbound, formless, and mysterious enjoyment where everything is as it is.

Mythological and Historical Accounts of Delphi, the Center of the World

Before the pantheon of gods and goddesses looked upon humanity and Earth from the heaven-world of Mount Olympus. there were only the primal divinities Chronos and Rhea (literally, Time and Flow). There were no other beings, for as soon as Rhea would give birth to a new form, Chronos would eat them, This mythology refers to a *time* when forms (particularly men and women) were entirely subject to time and determination, when there was no knowledge of fateful living, nor "authencity", nor the transcendence of the passing of forms.

Like all mothers, Flow wanted her offspring not to be consumed by Time, and so, on the birth of a new child she tricked Chronos by wrapping a large stone in swaddling clothes. Chronos ate the stone and the newborn escaped Time's hunger. The child, *Zeus* (Sanskrit *Dyas*, "Day/Sky/Brightness), who would give luminesce to the day's canopy, was thus born in a cave high on Mount Ida, Crete. He quickly grew to full power and banished his father, Time, who had meanwhile vomited the stone, to rule the *eternal* Fields of Elysium. (And up with the stone came also Zeus's previous brothers and sisters.)

Rhea, in substituting the stone for the child, also mothers the metaphor, giving rise to the dawn of symbology. To be *carried across* (*meta-phor*) time appears as the first conscious sacrifice, as the liberation of feeling indeed shatters Time's stranglehold on creation. Because of the giving of the divine Flow and liberation of feeling, there appeared a divine Brightness, and Chronos was, at last, resolved into eternity.

In the metaphor of the divine Flow, the seed of metaphysics was given genesis. Upon the sacred work (*sacri-fice*) of the Goddess, a luminosity that exceeds death appeared upon the land.

Zeus's Brightness from Rhea's perfect Flow is not only a poetic description, a mythological metaphor, and a historical moment, but indicates also an understanding whereby the revelation of the world (particularly epitomized as evolution) and the being of mankind (epitomized as each of us) began to learn of their bright and timeless transparency to one another. The mythic seed which flowered into non-mythic consciousness was glimpsed in the birth of Zeus.

Zeus first married Metis (Wisdom), and when she became pregnant, Gaia told Zeus that the infant of Metis was destined to be greater than that of the progenitor—so Zeus promptly swallowed Metis and embryo. This combining of power with wisdom *is* of the first order, eternity's first necessity in the affairs of gods and men. The embryo reappears later as Athena, born full-grown, suddenly mature. Indeed, the sharp and cunning Athenians overthrew the mythology with schools of philosophy.

Zeus then married Themis (Ordinance), and made the laws. Zeus, Brightness divine, stands above opposites and disputes—and the spirit-power of Zeus could be felt in the laws. With Themis, Zeus fathered Dike (Justice), the balanced Way between the means. Justice is the balance born from bright understanding. The marriage of Order and Brightness yielded a just and balanced rightness *(eudike)*.

Brightness loves to combine with all things, and Zeus is certainly no exception. Wandering in Tyre, he fell in love with the Phoenician princess Europa, and promptly appeared a a white bull—that which is strong, fearless, and good. He enticed Europa onto his back, pretending he was tame. But once upon the steed, Bright Zeus jumped into the sea and swam to Crete. Thenceforth, Europa of Tyre gave birth to Minos, leader of the Minoans, and became the motherly source of all her European grandchildren.

Through the mysterious gods we have learned how to rest with the unknowable, with the undefined, with perpetual growth and eternal life. And from the birth of gods, man and woman were called into and beyond themselves.

Even before the sanctuary was called Delphi, three thousand years ago, there were festivals and an oracle ceremony by the Cretan/Minoan priestesses worshipping Gaia, the great Mother. The sophistication of their religious ceremony had come as part of the lush growth of the Cretan-Minoan "thousand years of peace." The Minoan influence was found on the a small terrace and fountain upon the flanks of Parnassos, referred to then as *Pytho*, the *dragon* that would become *Delphi, womb*. Upon this high ground with its sweet fumes and holy spring, timeless words naturally spouted forth, a majestic beauty of inspired speech.

From this sacred place, divine knowledge quenched the thirst of pilgrims.

Zeus released two eagles—his own birds, from the opposite ends of the Earth, knowing that they would cross at the earth's center. This is how the location of Delphi, the sacred center was determined.

Zeus then send Apollo, his own son from the Northeast, to Delphi to claim the sacred center as a seat for his spiritual power. His passage from

Hyperborea carries the stories, mysteries, and understanding of the philosophy from the Northern shamans and mystics of India. It is this force that goes south and west to meet an elegance as the eagles cross at the center.

Guarding the sacred ground was a dragon-snake. Let us take a moment to consider the significance of the reptilian talisman. The snake simultaneously represents many forces. The shedding of the skin is, of course, a universal symbolism for renewal. But as a talisman, as a power in our evolutionary heredity, the snake represents the transition from worm to spine, from dim flesh to acute nervous system and spinal awareness. As a spinal metaphor, the snake is associated with a range of energies from fleshy pleasures to higher enjoyments, from sensual sexuality to mystic integration, from rushes of energy to deep rest. The whole range of energies, low and high, and the stillness of primal rest was anciently symbolized in its esoteric fullness by the caduceus (and the risen snake of the royal Egyptian headdress). Likened to the *kundalini* of the Indian yogis, all are esoteric indications of the nervous system in full unfoldment, inviting all to mystical openness in the unlimited divine.

Fascination by energies, gross or subtle is penetrated by Apollonian insight. It is the gift of Apollo to see the One Brightness in each of the many things and energies he encounters. Apollo represents the evolutionary discriminative leap beyond the limits of the nervous system.

So Apollo came to the center of the world and with his "silver tipped arrows" and his "phallus beams" slew the dragon-snake and fertilized the luxuriant ground. Apollonian discrimination claimed central position in the culture—a theological divinity beyond fascinations, clarifying and enlivening all that is seen.

Apollo then danced at the center, his fingers striking the strings of his lyre as the fullness of his radiance blessed the sacred center in beautiful song.

Delphi! Here I shall entertain
To build a far-famed
Temple and ordain
An Oracle to inform
the minds of men,
Who shall forever
offer to my love
The greatest gifts
—even all the men that move
In rich Peloponnesus and
all those of Europe, and the
isles the seas enclose,
Whom future search of Acts
and Beings bring—
To whom I'll prophesy the truths of things
In that rich Temple where my Oracle sings.

Apollo went north to purify himself for his killing of the Python, and, in his absence, mortals responded with a House and Sanctuary for the god who had mastered the serpent. (And it is Apollo's pet snake, the *coluber longissimus,* that twines around Asklepios' medical staff.)

In the Temple of Apollo, the ancient Goddess and mastered Snake continued in the form of the Oracle speaker, the Pythia, the Sybil of Delphi. This combination (in broad terms) of Minoan aesthetic genius and Dorian cunning power gave birth to an ecstatic "child". Suddenly, the active and receptive principles were equal divinities in which the world was both enjoyed and understood.

With the insertion of Apollo into the goddess culture, the snake became a womb, Pytho morphed into Delphi, was fertilzed, and a *theological* understanding was born from the now-illumined myths.

The Temple built to Apollo became the heart in the foundation of Western culture. The truth that penetrates all fascinations had claimed the center, and a theological understanding began to appear out of the myths.

And so it was told that after Apollo claimed the sacred center for his father, Zeus then took the stone with which sacrificial Rhea had diverted Chronos' attention and placed it there, beside the sacred spring on the terrace with its sweet gases. The Omphallos, the metaphorical diversion of Chronos, the seed of symbology, or navel-marker of the world, was placed by the timeless Brightness, marking Delphi as the spiritual center of the world.

The Omphallos was the part of the *mythos* which would grow into *logos* — indeed the Athenians called the Omphallos "the seed of *logos*." The discrimination that changes time to eternity and snake to openness was mythically germinated in the West at Delphi, and would give birth to a host of foundational Western contemplations.

Apollo spoke through the Pythia as she performed the Oracle between the two gods, Apollo and Dionysus. In honored and ceremonial worship the Pythia gave herself intoxicatingly (in the manner of Dionysus) to Apollo, and from this "marriage" there appeared a stillness beyond the storm of feeling, where she completed in her own flesh and spirit the dyad of submission and penetration. Her reflections to precious questions were appreciated as miraculous, an ecstatic appearance of the god Apollo — spoken through a bodily agent of the Goddess.

This "epiphany" could be witnessed and participated in on the seventh day of every spring, summer, and autumn month—nine times a year. Questions cast upon her miraculous pool were reflected back to the questioner with the flavor of immortality.

> *And the Sybil, with raving lips uttering things mirthless, unbedzened, and unperfumed, reaches over a thousand years with her voice, thanks to the divinity in her.*
> —*Herakleitos, 6th Century B.C.E.*

At the center of the temple was Zeus' birth stone, the Omphallos — the "original metaphor" —

as the navel-marker of the world. From this metaphor, all other metaphors were born, beginning with the metaphor of the gods.

The Omphallos received sacramental worship by the priests of Apollo, the *Prophetes*, in the center *adyton* where the Sybil or Pythia—witnessed by the timeless stone—would *utter forth* ("prophesy") the timeless words. In religious ceremony, the Omphallos was ritually adorned with woolen yarn, for it was said that when the goddess Harmonia wove the web of the world she started with the Omphallos at the center.

In the adyton, an eternal fire burned continuously for 1600 years, being extinguished but once by invaders. All fires throughout Hellas came from Delphi. It was considered an auspicious beginning to have the Oracle give a new colony a blessing prophecy for its future and coals from the eternal fire. It is said that a thousand cities around the Mediterranean began this way.

Although certainly not free of petty politics, at its peak Delphi was like no place in history, glistening with gifts, and hosted an Amphictony (a kind of "United Nations") for communication between the different city-states, all of whom wanted access to Delphi and the Oracle. The Amphictony (lit. "states around") were those twelve other districts surrounding the Delphic district of Hellas. These districts held a political and cultural forum at Delphi and adorned it with sumptuous gifts. The central calendar, coordinating religious festivals with a Pan-Hellenic schedule, as well as standardized rituals of purification and ceremony, came from Delphi. Thus, because of the Amphictony, the people of the lower Balkan peninsula came to forever call themselves "Hellenes," and their entire county "Hellas". (What the Romans *mistakenly* referred to as "Graecia" ("Gray," the name of one village). The "Greeks" are known to themselves as *Hellenes* and their county as *Hellas*.

Twenty seven centuries have passed since Delphi first held the Pythian games. What delineated the games at Delphi from the games of Olympia was that the Pythian competition also included the courting of the Muses. Emphasis on poetry, song, dance, and instrumentals elevated the championship contests to the higher arts.

Musiki was an exercise in resonance and anciently meant all the arts, not just music. Apollo and his lyre would lead and guide the inspiration and bless the Pythian games. While athletics were indeed celebrated, Apollo's Muses infused the competitions at Delphi with spirituality. It was, after all, the center of the world and the home of the Muses.

It is no accident that all the Muses are women—emphasizing the necessity and power of *reception* in the process of inspiration. The submission of the Muses to Apollo represented the intoxication of submission to the god of harmony.

What we call an "educated" or "distinguished" person, the ancients would address such as one as *musiki*. To be unmusical was, well, crude. The exercise of resonance (*harmonia*) was seen as *primary to* education and informed the student of the internal avenues of character, health, and understanding. So important was it that Plato declared that music should precede and dominate gymnastics, for the soul should form the body, not visa versa.

Yehudi Menuhin, in *The Music of Man*, gives this musical role of Delphi his highest praise:

> *There is surely no more impressive site in the world than the Temple of Apollo at Delphi on Mount Parnassus; of all the glorious holy places, this site of the Oracle of Delphi established the link between music and mystery.... The word music itself comes for the Greek word* musiki, *meaning all the arts of the nine Muses. Apollo, son of Zeus, was the leader of the Muses, as master athlete and warrior as well as master musician. Mount Parnassus came to be thought of as the home of music.*

Let it also be noted that the Temples and Treasuries at Delphi were the first Museums, temples holding art creating by those who had been taken by the Muses. To walk up the Sacred Way was to be immersed in beatitude, to be embraced by the artful glow of divine creation.

The golden age of ancient Hellas, which defined Western history, did not fall out of the sky, or come out of nowhere. It was given birth by the religious and spiritual understanding of the pre-Socratic, divine-worshipping priestesses, priests, *musiki*, Orphic mystics and raving ek-statics. Therefore, let us stand again upon the steps of Apollo's Temple and contemplate the divinities within the sacred space.

The Ecstatic Dance of Apollo and Dionysus

At Delphi, the sacred "Womb" and Heart of the ancient Hellenic world, *two* gods, Apollo and Dionysus, stood most resplendently in the Temple. What these gods represent individually, and in their relationship to each other, is a unique description of human growth, human understanding, and human ecstasy.

Ecstasy—the favor of the gods; from *ek-stasis*, "to stand out." But this is not necessarily a description of an "out-of-the-body" experience, an "astral projection," or even a frenzied pitch of religious or pagan fervor. For the purposes of discussion, let us speak of two complementary, yet partial, definitions for *ek-stasis*—mirroring the qualities of Dionysus and Apollo.

The first aspect refers to the "feeling" or "subjective" dimension. In this sense, to "stand outside oneself" is to commune with the life-feeling to the point that the feeling-enjoyment "outshines" the limitations of self. Every blessed dancer, lover, and bacchant knows what it is to be consumed, beyond even the fullness of ordinary pleasure to ecstatic enjoyment—where passion reaches the heart and the body is set free. Such raving is the rapture, visitation, and appearance of Dionysus.

The other aspect of *ek-stasis* has to do with the nature of awareness itself—"free" awareness as opposed to self-bound self-consciousness. Awareness that is bound to any point of view accepts the limitations of that definition. This point of view could be termed "centricity."

Centricity is the logic of locality and the myopia of position: from any point there is an observable logic to the rest of existence. From this presumption of position arises prideful *hubris* and the arrogance of power. (Thus, it is also said that we are philosophers of our adaptation.)

But we cannot accept any logic as truth unless the prison of centricity is ecstatically transcended, "stepped beyond" — shot with arrows or blended into the *harmonia kosmos*. Such is the appearance of the god Apollo with his stringed instruments, the lyre and bow. Apollo's golden lyre and silver bow and arrows represent the two ways to effect the transcendence of centricity. "Ego-centricity" in particular has great meaning, but the transcendence of centricity also has a social history.

The geocentric-to-heliocentric change beginning in the Renaissance marked a new culture. For Westerners, the understanding and transcendence of the cultism of Christianity, Eurocentricity, and mental/male centricity likewise marks a new age in history, but that is for a later discussion. For now let us just say that Apollonian ecstasy reveals the free awareness that is beyond centricity.

While ecstasy could be called a form of self-transcendence, it is not self-denial. In fact, the foundation for self-transcendence <u>is</u> a strong self. Like the eye above the foundational pyramid of self, ecstasy is the free awareness that stands upon (and beyond) definitions and limitations. Ecstasy is not something to be sought because of a bad or incomplete self-feeling. Rather than denying self, we simply locate ourselves in a process of growth that includes self, and accept any ordeal that this process requires. Self is not to be denied, but rather harmonically cultivated and then ecstatically understood. Likewise socially, each cult must locate itself in the same process of growth wherein the limits that create self-definition are exceeded and *culture* is created.

Ecstasy is an ancient Western word for the state and stage of life that no longer presumes the limits imposed by body, mind, self, and culture—even as it fully includes and embraces them. Sharing his or her enjoyment of what is limitless, an ecstatic naturally points out the limitations of the cult and culture from which he or she arose. No wonder the ancient Hellenic word for "witness" was *martyr,* a word-form that has remained essentially unchanged after thirty centuries.

Such is a partial description of ecstasy. Descriptions of expanded awareness and deep enjoyment of the divine nature of life are to be found in the heart of every culture. This growth process is described in countless cosmologies, and is archetypally portrayed in Western history in the dynamism of Dionysus and Apollo, the classic dyad of free feeling and harmonic wisdom.

Let us first focus on the elder Apollo, god from the Northeast (meaning India), god of intellect, wisdom, and foresight. The name Apollo intimates an understanding of his divinity. It has been suggested that its root is found in "*a-polla*," meaning "not of many." This would make sense since Apollo's cosmological function (with his bow and lyre) is that of harmonic penetration. Apollo sees the source brightness (the father day-brightness, *Zeus*) in every different thing, and also sees that the brightness is singular, or "not of many." It has also been similarly suggested with equal persuasion that the word Apollo comes from *apellei,* "gathering." This likewise rings true, as Apollo is the god of *logos*, the gathering of what has been set apart. *Logos* is to speak, to understand, to harmonically gather.

It was Apollo who led the Muses and consumed the Sibyl, the Seer, and the Pythia at Delphi. To realize or be visited by Apollo is to see and feel the divine creative Source gathered from every different thing, and let *logos* speak its truth.

"*The Wise is One Only. It is willing and unwilling to be called by the name 'Zeus.' If you have not heard me by all of this but Logos, then I can say: All is One.*" The words of Herakleitos echo loudly across millennia.

And a deeper memory of the divinity can be heard in the ancient Orphics (precededing *philosophia),* chanting Apollo's hymn with the full feeling that "Zeus" means "Brightness":

*ZEUS EVERYWHERE-ZEUS
EVERYWHERE-ZEUS EVERYWHERE.
Zeus the first, Zeus of the flashing lightning
bolt the last; Zeus the head, Zeus the middle,
from Zeus have all things been made. Zeus is
the foundation of the earth and of the starry
heaven; Zeus was male, Zeus was the
immortal bride; Zeus the breath of all things,
Zeus the rush of the flame unwearied; Zeus
the source of the sea, Zeus the sun and moon;
Zeus the king, Zeus of the flashing lightning,
the beginning of all things. For he concealed
all and again brought them forth from his
sacred heart to the glad light, working
wondrous things.
ZEUS EVERYWHERE-ZEUS
EVERYWHERE-ZEUS EVERYWHERE.*

Apollo, the divine son, is a discriminative insistence of the One great god, Zeus (the father-part of Apollo's own flesh), the supreme being. This insight is a penetrating one: Apollo's arrows are identical to the penetrating insight—divine, but not supremely so. The singular Brightness is supreme and begat not only insightful Apollo, but all things.

The Homeric Hymn to Apollo tells how the new-born god's very first action was to throw off his swaddling clothes and proclaim to the gods who had gathered, *"Please give me my beloved Lyre and Bow; I'll cast prophecy to men, and make them know Zeus's perfect counsel."*

Both the lyre and the bow depend on tension and release, the setting apart and the coming together, releasing beauty in the paradox of opposites. This single principle is described at the dawn of philosophy by Herakleitos as "a fitting together turned back on itself" in which "that which is drawn apart becomes one with itself as in the bow and lyre . . . Out of all things comes a unity, and out of a unity all things." (Let it be noted that in these instances, Herakleitos was probably restating common Orphic sayings.)

Apollo's penetrating intelligence makes him the god of harmonic wisdom. He represents the truth of philosophical endeavors, and is equally abundant in the poetic and musical arts as the leader of the Muses. He is seen with the silver bow and arrow, symbolizing the penetration of insight, and also with the golden lyre, which expresses the one harmony between different tones.

At Delos this god of wisdom stood gigantic in statuary repose, with the bow in his left hand and the Charites or Graces in his right hand, signifying, it was said, the seniority of graciousness over sharpness when the being is at rest. (And thus it was that his lyre was golden and his bow silver.)

Apollo shared the temple at Delphi with his resonant complement and younger half-brother

Dionysus, commonly known as the god of the vine and celebration. They both shared the Temple with more ancient altars to Gaia and Poseidon, honoring their Minoan roots. But Apollo and Dionysus were the active divinities of the Temple and were equal sons of the One Great Brightness, dyadic half-brothers of Father Sky. Delphi, the Center of the World, belonged to both gods, as told by Plutarch:

> *If anyone asks, "What has this to do with Apollo?," we shall say that it concerns not only him, but also Dionysus, whose share in Delphi is no less than that of Apollo.*

Where Apollo is wisdom, Dionysus is enjoyment. Where Apollo is active as transcendence, Dionysus is active as submission. Where Apollo is the insight that penetrates, Dionysus is the energy itself. Where Apollo is harmony, Dionysus is the sound. Where Apollo is spirited flesh, Dionysus is flesh in spirit. Where Apollo proclaims unity, Dionysus claims the multifarious energy of everything. Where Apollo (surnamed "Shoot From Afar") is clarity, Dionysus raves *(bacchos)*. Where Apollo discriminates, Dionysus worships. It is the dance of these two divinities that is the human dance of ek-stasy. Apollo is the ekstasy of vision, Dionysus is ek-static in feeling.

Delphi itself was something of an epiphany of these two gods: Apollo and the Muses on high

Parnassos, coming down halfway to meet pilgrims at "the sacred center" while Dionysus lived amongst the people, going up to Delphi. Dionysus' closeness to humanity was part of a deep human understanding, and the story of his life described for the people a developmental fabric of growth. The story of Dionysus gave man and woman a vision of simple beginnings and *supreme* pleasure, divine feeling. He was known as the god of ecstasy, and the story of his life is somehow duplicated in the life of every man and woman.

Therefore, let us focus in depth on this wine-god, Dionysus, whose *mysteries* provided essential understanding in the ecstatic foundations of Western culture. The Orphic story of the god of ecstasy is the story of how the divine feeling grows in man and woman and also beyond him and her. It is a great Western story of how mortals grow toward and into the immortal. As such, ecstasy is the Court of Olympia, the Dionysian entry into the royal epiphany of being and time, Being and timelessness.

Dionysus is the god of celebration, the god of wine, the god of the vine, the god of the life that is found in every living thing. His fuller name, Zagreus Dendrite Dionysus Eleutherios, is known by Orphic initiates of his mysteries. Each of his names refers to a stage of personal growth.

Zeus, the fertile god of brightness, is his father, and Semele, a Theban princess, his mortal mother. The great goddess Hera, Zeus's wife, was extremely jealous of her lover's wanderlust and tried to destroy the pregnant Semele. In her anger, Hera tricked Semele into asking Zeus to show her his true nature. When the god of infinite Brightness let himself be seen, Semele, a mere mortal, was consumed. But Zeus gathered the unborn child and put him into his own thigh. Soon after, Dionysus was born from Zeus's left leg (note: twice-born, once of flesh and once of spirit) into the hands of Hermes, who took him to his mother's family.

Hera was not fooled and sent the Titans to destroy the child. The Titans ripped Dionysus apart and ate his dismembered pieces. This is the origin of his first name, *Zagreus* (lit. "torn apart").

Zeus raged, hurled his bolts of lightning and reduced the Titans to ashes. It is said that out of those ashes humanity was born, so that although every man and woman may be full of that burnt Titanic strife, they also carry a spark of divinity within them always. Zagreus is thus the name of the divine spark within the field of Titanic anxiety, or faith within dark separativeness.

But the Titans had not consumed all of baby Dionysus. A sliver from his heart was saved and from it he was resurrected. Zeus again sent Hermes, the divine messenger, to take the young child to the forested Mt. Nysa to hide the baby from Hera's jealous rage. Hermes' role as messenger is incarnated countless times in the heroic journey of maturation. Who sends the messenger but the Source of All? Hermes not only brings the divine message, but also grants a celestial flight to a place where enjoyment grows from the faith.

(We know from other literary descriptions of Praxitiles' *Hermes and Baby Dionysus* that Hermes is dangling a bunch of grapes, attracting the infant wine-god with the promise of his destiny, and in his left hand (also) held his famous Caduceus, a *Hermetical* indication of the full unfoldment of the nervous system.)

To further conceal Dionysus from Hera when they arrived at Nysa, he was changed into a young goat.

The forest nymphs raised the young goat-Dionysus on the nectars of the forest. The satyrs (half-goat, half-man) taught him flesh-feelings, pleasure, and in time exuberant sexuality. The Muses taught him poetry, song, and dance, while the sileni (half-man, half-horse, found near the source of springs) taught him wisdom. Surrounded with such blessing and help, he grew quickly. During this growing period Dionysus, in the form of the young goat, was referred to as *Dendrite,* literally, "tree-youth". (Coincidentally, in anatomical terms, "dendrite" refers to the tree-like nerve endings, the "place" of pleasure, pain, and sensation. Indeed, the entire nervous system itself is tree-like.)

Dendrite spent his early years at Mt. Nysa until he was at ease with feelings from pain, fear, and wanting to pleasure, full-breath, and simplicity. Alive with native animal feelings, brimming with energy, flush in pleasure, full of breath, simple in countenance, his confidence was grounded in blessing as grandmother Rhea ("divine Flow"), Zeus' mother, the mother of brightness, then initiated the mature Dendrite into the *secret women's mysteries*. By her initiation, he was changed from his goat form back to his "human" and godly form, known everywhere as Dionysus, *dionysa,* the god of Nysa, a forest of celebration. Such holy baptism is the washing of all previous feeling with spirit. It is the ecstatic transition to divine feeling.

Rhea's key role in the divine transformation indicates how the divine flow or holy spirit must be yielded to in the manner of a goddess, not attained, "known" or conquered. Dionysus emerges from Dendrite in the midst of a divine submission and baptism, the secret women's mysteries. To advance beyond the stage of achievement and natural fullness is not another achievement, it is a submission. Thus it is said the transition from pleasure to ecstasy bridges the abyss between self and sacrifice.

Now a delighted god, Dionysus' power was complete. He continued to grow in enjoyment and power as he cut a swath of wild and joyous celebration across the land, accompanied by the free-pleasuring Satyrs, the raving Maenads, the wild women who had been initiated by him, and also by anyone who would join them.

Dionysus and his joyous party taught ecstatic celebration (and wine-making) in village after village, town after town. On his way to Athens, he paused and celebrated at the Mt. Kitheron town of *Eleutherea,* and then to *Eleusis,* where his celebrations were completely free.

Emerging from the mysteries of Eleutherea and Eleusis, he took the name *Eleutherios*, meaning both "from Eleutherea" and "the Liberator." He entered Athens, celebrated with wine, and told his story, leading everyone into ecstasy. Below his statue at his Temple at the Theatre in Athens, the name Dionysus does not appear at all—only the name *Eleutherios*.

For the months of winter, a cycle of four Dionysian festivals was central to the ancient religious calendar. The first of these was near the winter soltice, and the climax of this cycle was the Great Dionysia,

near the spring equinox, where the people of Athens reenacted the story of Dionysus. The first day's liturgies involved a priest leaving Temple Eleutherios at sunset with a *xoanon,* an icon of the god. It was the god personified, going to Eleutherea, the place where his celebration is completely free.

Just as the priest passed out of the Dipylon (Double) Gates, people would jump out from hiding and recapture the god. The wine-filled crowd would sing songs of thanksgiving and celebration, for the god was still with them; but Dionysus, in the form of the priest and icon, sang of his longing to go to the place where he could freely be. Only then did he consent to his petitioners and bless them with delight for another year.

"The rich robes were the most beautiful part of the whole festival. The statue was seated in a festival car, drawn by two men dressed as the attendant sprites of Dionysus. Sitting on either side of the statue were two men playing flutes. Ahead of them were two youths bearing branches, another with a basket and a fourth with a censor from which incense perfumed the air. At the very beginning was another youth with a trumpet. Then the return over the same route originally travelled by Dionysus was made in the dark, lighted by the flaming torches which illuminated the faces of the celebrants. Thus the god was brought back to his theatre, at a point near his temple, so that he might be present during the festivals at all performances and dithyrambs . . . [These] songs of revelry to the god Dionysus, were sung to the musical accompaniment of the flute."

The parade returned the priest and icon to the Temple of Dionysus Eleutherios and the entire celebration became part of the story itself. At the end of the procession, the god was re-installed in the Temple in a celebratory religious ceremony, then everyone gathered on the curved hillside below the Acropolis for the dramatic and musical story telling of the life of Dionysus.

Under the reign of Peisistratos (influenced heavily by Onomakritos, Court Seer and famous Orphic Rhapsodist and initiator), the people marbled the seats on the curved hillside below the Acropolis of Athens. Such honoring of the Orphic telling of Dionysus is the appearance of public theatre in the Western world.

Theatre — Satyr -> Bakhos
Theatre is the transfomation
of the goat into the god

The play was originally called "*tra-godia*" or "goat song", for it is the story of how we grow from torn-apart to a satyr, then from pleasure to ecstasy.

Zagreus-faith changes to the Dendritic goat, who grows until the god of the forest appears in submission: *Dionysus*, 'the god of Nysa'. These transformations of Dionysus are the primary dramas for everyone: the transformation of the torn-apart back to growing enjoyment and the goat into the god.

The sensation of feeling separate from others, from everything, even from oneself, is what was known in the mystery schools as *Zagreus*, "torn apart." And yet they also noted an inextinguishable spark even in the darkest of individuals and times. That flicker is the night sparkle, the divinity surrounded with fear and titanic anxiety. Unextinguishable, the spark grows in faith until there is a transition to enjoyment, as the divine messenger Hermes (surnamed "Crosser of Boundaries") takes you to Nysa. There, sensuality and enjoyment grow until feeling is free. From embryonic development to full unfoldment, Hermetical wisdom communicates about the Orphic passage through fear and pleasure to the ecstasy beyond mortality.

How is this done, or begun? By living a life of delight, pleasure, and enjoyment to whatever degree we can lovingly dare, and simultaneously entering into an ordeal of responsible observation whereby the limits on that enjoyment are truly noticed.

At first, these limits will most certainly be emotional in nature. Sin, guilt, shoulds and shouldn'ts, mommy and daddy, absurd and *anxious* rationalizations of all kinds (real and imagined), appear at the edge of our Dionysian pleasure. At last, even the limits of the nervous system are relaxed beyond. At first, delusion, adolescence, capriciousness, arrogance, degeneracy, and narcissism of all kinds appear at the edge of our Apollonian observation. At last, mystery exceeds all knowledge. It is the task of each responsible participant to uncover and grow beyond what he or she must in order to let *being* stand in the place where animals, children, and clever adolescents stood before.

The most difficult phase of growth is the Dendrite phase. Growing up is more of a struggle than any other transition. It is not just the continual flowering of greater and greater enjoyment, surrounded by forest nymphs and the muses. The exploration of animal feelings, its fullness and its limits, its fleshiness, pleasures, and memory, is reflected in another appellation/surname of Dendrite-Dionysus: *Chthonios*, "underground force." Drinking from the well of flesh-feelings also carries a deep memory of death and deep-seated fear. The passage through the dark comes with the pleasures of the flesh.

There is real labor enduring the revelation of dark unconsciousness. When hard labor is required, *Chthonios* feels his shoulder pressed against the plough of his/her necessary work. As (s)he turns old ground anew, the acceptance of the task soon dawns into another reality. What (s)he uncovers through the work becomes the field of enjoyment.

Chthonios was also a surname for Apollo. The mysteries were his, he taught humans how to use the darkness, he revealed the passage to the Lord of Death. To one who is immersed and incubated in the underground force, it is Apollo who reveals his father, the Bright Immortal in all mortal things, places, and beings.

And while Hermes also guides souls through the underworld, he cannot toil or decide for them. Sometimes Dendrite/Dionysus is forever chthonically plowing, sometimes forever lying in the field.

But the growth and transformation of Dendrite is centered in becoming. This process is observed and felt in time as the pleasure that was, the enjoyment that will be, the incompleteness of the present. But limitations in enjoyment can be felt for their self-createdness, the tension of the Titans, the opposite of Rhea's baptism. Future *tense*. Past *tense*. Present *tense*. In the process of this recognition, time is only a tension added to this enjoyment, this moment. This tension harbors the past, the future, the incompleteness of the present, and obscures being into becoming.

The more this tensing is recognized, the more one can return to the presence (beyond even the present tense), and, in the baptism of Rhea's submission ("divine flow"), Dionysus suddenly appears as always being there. He enters the present by recognizing the added tensing, but *stays* present by the power given to him from whatever he delights in, in whatever he allows to be and blesses. Apollo's arrows shoot through self-tension and, letting a native shine appear, as awe comes from everything. Present feeling and enjoyment overflows (Rhea) the Dendrite body and blends into what surrounds him; he or she is *ek-static*. His or her intimacy with the divine washes the tension of time previously and unconsciously added to the presence. Dionysus lies, while alive, in the Fields of Elysium.

This intoxication becomes a swoon, and in the middle of the swoon, like a calm in the middle of a storm, like a simplicity in chaos, appears a clearing, the resolution of "I" into free feeling; no separate self and no other, but free feeling only, the feeling that is universal. In that clearing, sight becomes the light it always was and speaks in visions and of simplicity. Language itself issues the name, *Eleutherios*. Free feeling is the Western Liberation, the unfolding truth that sets us free.

The association of the satyr with the foundation stage of the god is the "primary theater." The Zagreus stage need only be *hermetically* recognized and it is soon past. Eleutherios comes by grace. But the Dendritic transition and the passage through the underworld is the ordinary toil of becoming a man or a woman. Fortunately, we have religious ancestors who understood celebrations as a practice of growth in sacred enjoyment, beyond the reaction to the chthonic. The spiritual necessity of free pleasure was valued in a culture whose central Temple held the god of celebration.

But Dendrite does not become ecstatic by the enjoyment principle alone. Dionysus stands in the Temple of *Apollo* in Delphi. On the wall in the temple is written Apollo's two famous sayings: ΓΝΟΘΙ ΣΕΑΤΟΝ, and ΜΕΔΑΝ ΑΓΑΝ, *"Gnothi Seaton"* and *"Medan Agan"*—commonly known as "Know thyself" and "Nothing in excess."

The way we moderns consider "know thyself" was cast as far back as Socrates as an internal process of self-discovery, implying or leading to the soul or transcendental Self. But this was not the original meaning as inscribed upon the Temple walls. To the priests and Sages who preceded the logical obsession, *"Gnothi seaton"* was closer to "Know thyself to be human and follow the god" or divine feeling. This sage advice was not directed only at an internal world of self-revelation, but was the necessary wisdom needed to counter the force of *hubris,* or pride. *"Gnothi Seaton"* conveyed an understanding of an individual accepting the unknowable infinity within which he or she inheres, and thus not fall prey to false pride, knowledge, or other limitations of the developing self. And *"Medan agan"* could be more clearly translated as "Do not leave the middle," from which it is easy to see the usual, more shallow translation, "Nothing in excess." One can almost recall the letters upon the temple,

ΓΝΟΘΙ ΣΕΑΤΟΝ
ΜΕΔΑΝ ΑΓΑΝ

The "growth" of being is always a dance of the Dionysian and Apollonian strengths. The Dionysian pleasure, energy and feeling is full of "life's native urge to ecstasy." That urge is guided, drawn, and husbanded by the senior principle of Apollonian harmony and wisdom, or else the Dionysian passion becomes a blind, self-destructive fury. We must submit to delight, feeling, pleasure, raving raggedness—and also discrimination, a critical eye, self-understanding, and self-discipline.

It was said that Dionysus so freely gave himself up that when he looked into a mirror, he was scattered across the universe. Apollo's "seniority" is expressed in his title, "Dionysus saviour." It is a description of the Apollonian "not-of-many" divine vision whereby all the "sparkles," or pieces of the god, or individuals, are seen as they are, not separate, but eternally alive in the body of the One Brightness. Glimpsing this singularity and growing into the One is said to be the re-membrance of the god once dismembered by titanic forces. Apollo represents the straight and harmonic lines that radiate from Zeus, the divine Brightness, and meets Dionysus, in the form of each man and woman, who is the life that grows.

When one's feeling grows from the Zagreus-spark within to the full pleasure of Dendritic skin, one becomes *flush* with enjoyment, being the body/mind/self/flesh without recoil or judgments. Then the body-flush becomes full in a radiant life-feeling;

this "glow" is the fruit of the Dendrite stage. *It is the narrow gate of the whole body.* This countenance is baptised most tangibly in a mysterious intercourse with the infinity within which we all mysteriously appear. Such is the appearance of Rhea, the flowing goddess. The Apollonian observation and penetration of the unconsciousness that presumes separation completes the vibrant life with transcendent light; and Dionysus, or the life-feeling that is built upon and greater than full pleasure, appears from within and steps out. Ecstatic feeling and delight continue to grow in a dance of wisdom and passion until feeling becomes free (Eleutherian), and blends into and becomes identical to the Feeling that is universal. "I" relaxes into awareness itself, not like a god looking from one's eyes, but from all eyes.

Consider the words of Macrobius:

> *In their Mystery-tradition Dionysus is represented as being torn limb from limb by the fury of the Titans, and after the pieces have been buried, as coming together again and whole and one. By offering itself for division from its undivided state, and by returning to the undivided from the divided, this Dionysian process both fulfills the duties of the cosmos and also performs the mysteries of its own nature.*

The ending of this quotation—"this Dionysian process both fulfills the duties of the cosmos and also performs the mysteries of its own nature"—is quite interesting. What is it to fulfill the duty of the cosmos while performing the mysteries of your own nature? The unfoldment of Zagreus Dendrite Dionysus Eleutherios represents the growth and fulfillment of man, woman, and "the mysteries of your own nature." So let us look at this process for the fulfillment of any cosmic duties.

Because of the unarmormed willingness to allow all feeling, Eleutherios sees the essence of things. He sees his body as a mound of all previous life, blending into his surroundings and all others. He thus sees through time in a kaleidoscopic cascade of archetypes. His reflective sensation of "me" resolves into awareness itself. Not disappeared, rather simply resolved in the transparency to primal light. Such a stage of development indicates the event whereby the Life that has grown for billions of years recognizes itself, transparently—fulfilling the duties of the cosmos. In such stillness, the ecstatic dance of Apollo and Dionysus is complete, and from their Temple the view is clear, resolving the past, the future, and even the present into *Epoptai,* the sacred Beholding of Presence, supreme Being.

The Oracle at Delphi

Of the ten sibyls in the ancient world, the most notable was the Pythia, the one through whom Apollo spoke timeless words at his Temple at Delphi. Nowhere was the possession of the gods more predictable or observable than watching the Sibyl of Delphi be taken by the god Apollo then rave responsively to the petitions of pilgrims. The Oracle was a regularly visible mystery, an observable portal of divine descent which blessed all Hellenes.

While the miraculous and mystery have an unknowable, unexplainable dimension, mythic explanations about the Oracle do not satisfy our discursive mind. We long for a trans-mythic, discriminative and theological appreciation of Western civilization's central mystery – and by coming to this apprehension, we understand ourselves more deeply.

As we traverse this Sacred Way, we will rest and dance with many paradoxes, *gnosis* and mystery, mortality and immortals, possession and authenticity, being and time, wonderful madness and logical visions. Appreciating the Oracle of Delphi, we have a lens to view ancient mysteries, original theology, and the formless understanding that integrates everything.

The Oracle's awe and power was evident in the framing of laws, the founding of colonies, the making and unmaking of kings, the beginning of wars, the healing of disease and pestilence and in the personal counsel to countless individuals for almost two millennia.

The ceremony was held in such high regard that Plato praised the rites and mystery at Delphi in the superlative. Plato (Rep): "For Apollo of Delphi will remain the most important, the noblest, and the chiefest acts of legislation .... the erection of temples, and the appointment of sacrifices and other ceremonies in honor of gods and demi-gods and heroes, and again the modes of burial of the dead, and all the observances which we must adopt to propitiate the denizens of the other world ... For it is this god, I presume, expounding from his seat by the Omphalos at the earth's centre who is the national expositor on such matters."

While it did not provide a political unity for the many peoples that made up the Hellenes, Delphi did function as the unifying ground of cultural and religious understanding. The examples and prominence of oracular sayings in the history of Hellenic destiny are well numerated, and its presence pervades mythological and literary expressions. Indeed, the keeping of dated time in the West was in Olympiad -- which, like many other historical moments, began in response to the utterance of Apollo at Delphi.

But what was this ceremony? What do we know about the oracle itself? How do we properly understand *entheos,* "divine possession" -- the proposed intercourse of humans and the gods?

"Oracle" is rooted in the Latin *oraculum,* a place of oracles, which, in turn, is further rooted in *orare,* to pray or plead. But the Oracle at Delphi is not a Roman mystery, but a Hellenic one, and the Hellenic word for oracle is *mantike. Mantike* shares etymological ground with *manna, manic,* mantic, and *mantis* (as in praying mantis, and *mantis* is the ancient Hellenic word for an inspired seer). All of these lexiconical cousins intimate an infusion, an *entheos,* a spirited possession, like when a dancer becomes the music. It is most interesting to note that in all of these words this "infusion" is nuanced by madness, or the enthusiastic loss of ordinary mind. Indeed, the ravings of the Pythia were described by Plato (Phaedo 244B) as *"mantike entheos."*

Let us also keep in mind that Apollo, the god of harmony and insight with his lyre and bow, not only penetrates the Pythia at Delphi, he leads the (feminine) muses -- goddesses that emphasize the role of receptivity in the process of inspiration and creativity.

In passionate and mindless submission to the Apollonian divinity of harmony and insight, the dancer, musician, poet, and oracular *mantis* gain the stillness that is ecstasy's gift. In the intoxicated flight of harmonic surrender, wisdom mysteriously shines clear and calm, like the still eye of a great storm. It is the peace beyond all knowing, spoken of in esoteric circles as utter stillness, *hesychia* -- which lets, witnesses, and allows all and includes all. Stillness is present to the dark and the light, to the dance and the silence, to being and time.

Via "incubation", *egkoimesis*, there comes a profound stillness and openness; we make room for the heart in depth, and thus we make room for the god. Stillness before inspiration, stillness before creativity, stillness before uncaused joy. Anyone who has danced freely, spoken poetically, contemplated the ground of being, or played an instrument with beauty knows the stillness and *harmonia* of Apollo.

At Delphi, on the seventh day of every month, excepting the three winter months when Apollo was away atoning for his slaying the serpent (*drakon*) at ancient Pytho. By slaying the reptilian automaticities, the god of insight and harmony, changed Pytho to Delphi. Via Apollo, the dragon-snake changed into a fertile womb.

Within this *delphys*, or womb, a woman would conduct an honored sacramental worship to Apollo. In intoxicated adoration to the god of harmony and penetration, the Pythia sat upon her tripod and breathed the sweet fumes coming out of the earth. She became ecstatic and impregnated, and in her fullness, would birth prophesy in response to questions.

Even the greatest intellectuals of the ancient world acknowledged the greatness of Delphi's sublime ceremony. "The raving Sybil, through the god , utters somber, unembellished and unperfumed sayings, reaching over a thousand years with her voice," Heraklitos proclaimed around the 70th Olympiad. (2500 years ago) From Plato to Plutarch and Aeschylus to Pindar the praise for the *mantike* (divine madness) at Delphi came with hearty superlatives.

From this ritual and other religious ceremonies and revelations, the recognition of a higher awareness appeared, but was often explained in mythic form, "the god took me," "the Muse took me," "Apollo came and spoke through me". (Let us recall that the Athenians called the omphallos at Delphi, "the seed of logos.") But a theological explanation for the divine process superceded the merely mythic one, and from this love of wisdom, philosophy was born. From these mystic, trans-mythic descriptions of supreme being and the One reality were founded and beheld the Apollonian transformation of mythos into logos.

At Delphi, <u>Zeus</u> was the voice heard by mortals, as Apollo was called, "the mouthpiece of Zeus." The Pythia channeled Apollo and Apollo channeled his Bright (*Zeus*) father.

The Oracle or *Mantike* was conducted as an intoxicated wedding celebration between the opened

Pythia and Bright Apollo. As the ceremony reached its acme and consummation, petitioners, through priests, could cast their concerns upon her rapture, and receive reflections of their future in her ravings.

The Pythia was classically a young virgin, from the precient of Delphi, chosen by the priests of Apollo, the *Prophetes*, not for her religious training nor for her position in a familial lineage, but for her simplicity and depth of feeling. For her time as a bride of Apollo, she lived as a celibate renunciate in a sisterhood of Delphic women who tended the eternal sacred fire in the temple, and was cared for as a vessel awaiting the divinity.

Plutarch tells us that her retreat and preparation freed her soul from all pertebation so that she could give herself to the god without reservation. We can imagine that she would allow her body, emotions, and mind a deep rest because she knew that a clear mind and open heart would combine with divine forces of Apollo's Temple. This worship was a luminous, lightning exchange and meeting of heaven and earth, an epiphany of awe and inspiration. The full submission of the mind to invocation and openness, of the body to enjoyment, the breath to fullness, and the heart to the god would cause a miracle to appear. A clear pool of awareness, unblemished by social tensions, or distractions in body and mind, would come forth and reflect what was cast upon it as perfectly as she could surrender to the calm itself. There, immersed and stilled in beatific adoration and intoxication, the god spoke in bright reflection.

The priestess of Delphi prepared for her wedding by fasting for three days, then on the night preceding her nuptials, she slept on a bed covered with Apollo's laurel leaves, and upon arising, bathed in the cold waters of Kastalia. She dressed in purple wedding attire and additionally empowered herself by carrying a branch of Apollo's prophetic laurel (*mantis daphne*) in her right hand. She drank from the holy waters sweetly

spouting from Kassotis, then entered the Sacred Way. Opened, pure, and exhilarated, she delighted in the world's finest demonstrations of statuary and jewelry as she rose past endless masterpieces of jewelry, paintings, statuary, dedications, musicians, songs, and the laurel of pilgrims to Apollo's Temple, ready to be taken.

In hallowed solemnity, the Pythia entered the core of Apollo's Temple, the sacred *adyton*, her sweet-smelling chamber, and took holy waters to purify her. Her eyes fell transfixed upon the golden statuary of Apollo and she imagined the brightness coming upon her. But first, she gazed upon the Altar to Dionysus, the eternal fire, Rhea's omphallos, altars to the Earth Ge and Sea Poseidon and her tripod spanning the cleft in the floor. She excitedly inhaled the sweet odor (*eudoia*) rising from the deep crack in the floor (*chasma*).

The priests of Apollo, the *Prophetes*, waved small torches of herbs and incense and engaged in rituals of anointment and decoration centered around the omphallos, the the stone which gave Zeus his own birth.

Upon the hearth of Hellas, the Altar to Hestia, she ritually gave the "never dying fire" her own sacred offerings of herbs, leaves, barley meal, and incense. Sweet smokes combined with the sweetness of the Earth's perfume, and having completed her preparation, the Pythia mounted her three-legged throne over the sacred fissure of Mother Earth. She inspired *Ge*'s breaths (*ge pneuma),* and they inspired her. She reportedly bent over the Sacred Stone, chewed

a laurel leaf and inhaled the vapors that were emitted from the chasm. Intoxicated and in awe, she entered a state of ecstasy, and when questioned, uttered amazing words of truth.

These vapors rose from the intersection of two fault lines (Scientific American, July 13, 2003), and was reported to be a sweet-smelling gas, whose fumes produced exhilaration and intoxication. According to Plutarch (CE 46-120), the Pythia was like a runner after a race or a dancer after an ecstatic occasion, and that after her intercourse with Apollo, she continued in calm and peace.

Plutarch, in addition to his famed role as biographical travelogue, retired at Delphi as a priest of Apollo, a *Prophetes*. Indeed, he became head (*epimeletes*) of the Amphictyonic council during the reign of Hadrian. We are grateful to him not only because he gives us a rational point of view on the workings of the oracle, but also subjective appreciations as well. He described the interrelationship of Apollo, the Pythia, and the vapors by likening the god to a musician, the woman to his instrument and the *pneuma* to the plectrum with which he touched her to make her speak. But Plutarch emphasized that the *pneuma* was only a trigger. It was really the preconditioning of the chosen woman that made her capable of responding to exposure to Earth's sacred breath. An ordinary person could detect the smell of the gas without passing into an oracular trance.

Only the sacred woman would conduct the god, if the god would give his assent. That willingness to come was determined by the nervous system of a sacrificial goat. Oracle priests brought a live goat-kid beside the Pythia and sprinkled it with cold water. If the kid shivered from the cold water it was taken as a strong sign that it would be an auspicious day for divination, and smiles broke across every face. The goat-kid was taken outside and sacrificed for a holy meal to show the crowds that the god had smiled upon the day.

Perhaps the goat's spirit was not lost. In her expanded state, the priestess could absorb the spirit of the goat's quiver up her own excited nervous system. Her charged spine would indicate that the Python, slain by the arrows of Apollo, was now resurrected as the Pythia—whose expanded and harmonious nervous system could resonate in concert to the lyre of Apollo. She was animal, human, and divine, a threefold epiphany, and all the goddess cultures which preceded her sang through her as men, cities, and empires bowed to her counsel, or suffered their own choices and myopia.

Whoever wished to consult the Oracle was obliged to pay a tax, the *telono*, which gave him the right to approach the great altar of Apollo to offer sacrifices (boars, goats or bulls). It was duly noted that the gift of the god was preceded by the gifts and gratitude from the people. The ceremony was an exchange, a relationship, not merely magic or solitary comprehension.

Petitioners stepped into the ante-room with great gratitude and sobriety. For the Pythia's words were clear: "Stranger, if pure of soul, enter into the sanctuary of the god of purity, having but touched the sacred stream. For lustration is an easy matter for the good. As for the wicked man, not the whole ocean with its waves could wash him clean."

The *Prophetes*, Priests of Apollo, Interpreters and Keepers of the *Mantike*, surrounded her, anointed the omphallos with ceremonial oils, served her in song and chant in her marriage to Apollo, so that she may respond to questions with his divine words. Through their combined devotion, ritual sacraments, and mutual awe, the marriage ceremony came to its consummation as the purpled-attired bride let herself fully go. And yet, she reached over, grasped a woolen thread around the omphallos to her left, for in her right hand she still held Apollo's aromatic laurel branch. Relinquishing all else, with deep breaths she gave herself like a lover entirely to the service of the god.

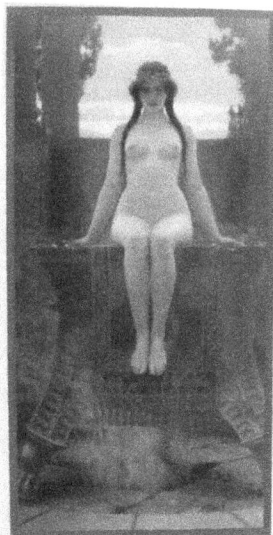

Petitioners stood just outside the *adyton* (lit. *no entry*) in an ante room, where the smells and sounds of the earth's center could nevertheless be closely appreciated. They were to wait in gratitude, aligned to the truth. For "the temples of the gods are thrown open to all good people, nor is there any need of purification. No defilement can ever touch virtue. But whoso is baneful of heart, withdraw; for the washing of the body will never cleanse the soul."

The *adyton,* the sacred chamber, was protected like a bridal suite, and only those of sacred intent and training were allowed within (wedding party only).

Once the Pythia was fully ecstatic and possessed, a *Prophetes* relayed to her the questions of petitioners, to which the Pythia, opened to the son of *Zeus*, raved his responses. These anointed words, *chresmon logos,* were interpreted by the *Prophetes*, who recorded her raving and passed it back to the questioner (often with a translation/interpretation).

Except for a brief moment during an invasion, the "eternal fire" upon Apollo's hearth was kept burning continuously for almost 1600 years, regularly re-lighting every other Temple in the land and lighting the fires of over a 1000 new colonies. We can assume that Delphi's ceremonial intoxication as an avenue to inspirational wisdom informed the Hellenes for at least that long, and there is archeological evidence and lore that supports a much longer worship.

Certainly, the enigmatic nature of the "anointed words" contributed to their prophetic significance. "The divine one whose oracle is in Delphi speaks neither directly or obscurely, but gives a sign," Heraklitos emphasized. But there is more to such a ceremony than enigma and myth, evidenced by the clear understanding grew from the words of a divine ceremony. While Delphi was not always free of corruption, it behooves us to look upon the *Mantike*'s great legacy to get our own first hand view of its divine character.

Fortunately, set collections of the oracles existed in ancient times, none of which survive, but are quoted from extensively.

As theology's rationalism began to have its widespread influence upon the land, the Oracle continued to "prove itself" to emerging rational minds. Two reports of Herodotus addressed this concern for validity.

*****

It was said that King Croesus wanted to test the veracity of the renown oracles, Delphi, Dodona, Branchidae, Zeus Ammon, Trophonius and Amphiaraus. He sent emissaries simultaneously to each of the holy sites, and they were to petition each oracle on the hundredth day from their departure as to the present activity of King Croesus. He spent that day boiling "the hard-shelled tortoise and the flesh of a lamb, with brass above and bath below."

Four oracles failed. Amphiaraus gave an excellent approximation, but the Pythia, reports Herodotus, not only knew the answer, but the mind of the questioners. As the Lydian emissaries were walking up the Sacred Way, they were confessing to one another their own doubts about the reality of the Oracle ceremony, but as they entered the Temple, before they could even ask their question, the Pythia screamed out, "I know the number of the sands and the dimensions of the sea / I understand the mute, and hear those who do not speak. / Into my head comes the shell of the strong-shelled tortoise." (Herodotus, 1.47.3). The pleased king responded with rich gifts.

King Croesus, having convinced himself that he could trust Delphi's ceremony, then asked the *Mantike* what would happen if he went to war with Cyrus. The oracle gave the famous reply, "Croesus by crossing the Halys would destroy a mighty kingdom." The ambiguity of the prophesy was not seen by the arrogant King and he followed his own *hubris*, did go to war with Cyrus, and indeed a great kingdom fell, his own.

Equally famous was the interpretation by Themistocles of the Pythia's words, "...wide eyed Zeus gives to the Triton-born a wooden wall to be alone impregnable .... thou shalt yet live to fight another day... O Salamis divine...." Themistocles interpreted "the wooden walls" to refer to ships, and counselled the Athenians to prepare for a fight at sea. "Divine Salamis" proved to be the salvation of Hellas, and the Athenians offered the first fruits of that battle to Delphi.

Perhaps the most celebrated historical person at Delphi was the immortal Pindar. Indeed, while Pindar lived, the revered madness, *mantike,* bade the Delphians that *equal* share of all the first-fruits offered to Apollo should go to the great poet, and a permanent chair was installed for him to sit in and recite his poems when he visited. In return, like generations of great poets, Pindar sang praises to gods and men, to victors in the Pythian Games, to Kings. Fortunately, we can still drink in a bit of Pindar's Pythian Odes, imagining the words of the Master poet ringing with depth and vision.

Golden lyre,
rightful joint possession of Apollo and the violet-
haired Muses,
to which the dance-step listens,
the beginning of splendid festivity,
and singers obey your notes
whenever, with your quivering strings,
you prepare to strike up chorus-leading preludes.
You quench even the warlike thunderbolt of
everlasting fire.

And the eagle sleeps on the scepter of Zeus,
relaxing his swift wings on either side ...

Grant that we may be pleasing to you, Bright Zeus,
you who frequent this mountain,
this brow of the fruitful earth,
whose namesake city near at hand was glorified by its
renowned founder, when the herald at the Pythian
racecourse proclaimed the name of Aetna,
announcing Hieron's triumph with the chariot.

Muse,
hear me,
and beside Deinomenes sing
loud praises for the reward of the four-horse chariot.
The joy of his father's victory is not alien to him.
Come,
 let us devise a friendly song for the king...

If you speak in due proportion,
twisting the strands of many themes into a brief
compass,
less blame follows from men.
For wearying satiety blunts the edge of short-lived
expectations,
what the citizens hear secretly weighs heavy on their
spirits,
especially concerning the merits of others.

Nevertheless, since envy is better than pity, do not
abandon fine deeds! Steer your men with the rudder
of justice;
forge your tongue on the anvil of truth.
If even a small spark flies,
it is carried along as a great thing
when it comes from you.
You are the guardian of an ample store.
You have many faithful witnesses of both good and
bad.

But abide in a blossoming temper,
if you are fond of always hearing sweet things
spoken of you,
do not be too distressed by expenses,
but, like a steersman, let your sail out to the wind.

Do not be deceived, my friend, by glib profit-seeking.
The loud acclaim of renown that survives a man
is all that reveals the way of life
of departed men to storytellers and singers alike.

*****

The oracle at Delphi was consulted and highly
honored by our Hellenic ancestors for a thousand years.
It was the exalted voice from the center of the world, a
place of access to the divine domain. But neglect and
Imperial Christianity caused the pagan temples to fall
into disrepute and silence. In 364 CE, Julian attempted

to revive the ancient Greek life and religion and sent his doctor and best friend, Oribasus, to Delphi, to try and invoke the Oracle again. Indeed, Apollo spoke prophesy once more, but only to announce its own end. "Tell the fair king," said the divinity through the Pythia, "to earth is fallen the deft-wrought dwelling/ no longer hath Phoebus shelter, or prophetic laurel/ or speaking fountain/ yea, the speaking water is quenched." Such was the last utterance of the Oracle, the death song of the ancient religion.

Let us not continue to dismiss such avenues of renown just because of their use of intoxicants and mythic wrappings. Let us note: While a few intoxicants held sacramental importance in our sacred history, our forerunners were balanced in the freedoms of pleasure by their love of wisdom. The non-sacred use of certain "potions", *pharmakon, ambrosia, pneumas,* and "nectars" was highly taboo. Because of their frequent use in the journey to the underworld, *hades,* "the unseen," only a rare and holy use of these intoxicants was wisely and socially permitted. When this law is violated and the sacrament abused, the profane are often captured by *hades* and litter the streets in delusion.

Intoxicants have an intimate place, but not a primary significance, in the sacred practices of western civilization, both at Eleusis and Delphi, as well as in many cultures all over the world, in every time. Plutarch explicitly made the point that it wasn't the *pneuma* but the devoted preparation that made the divinity appear. Sacramental use of intoxication such as at Delphi are to be understood, neither believed and exploited, nor doubted and discarded. It is the fool in every culture who confuses the sacrament and divinity. (And it is a greater fool who proclaims there is no ground or infinity.)

Certainly, we must not confuse sacraments and divinity, just like we must discern truth and fact. For it is discernment that is our real advantage, for it cuts the path from belief to understanding. Facts, like myths, are only partial forms and must be winnowed to give revelation in depth. The truth of understanding stands out as encompassing the formless and forms, the unreasonable and the perfectly logical, being in everything and in no thing. Soberly and in madness, we need only come to a clear invocation of the joy at the core of everything and give up everything for This.

The Caduceus, "Temple Sleep," and the Religious Origins of Western Medicine

Every medical student knows that Hippocrates is the father of Western medicine, and that the symbol of the snake around the staff is called the caduceus. But few can say what kind of medicine Hippocrates practiced, and fewer still know the significance of the serpentined staff.

Hippocrates, a contemporary of Socrates, was the exalted healer who lived in Hellas at the dawning of the Golden Age. As a healer, Hippocrates was known as an *Asklepiades,* or son of Asklepios (L. Aesclepios). At times, he was undoubtedly referred to as *Hippocrates Asklepiades,* with his last name indicating his trade, much like *Smith.* Imbued in his Hellenic healing tradition, Hippocrates carried "the staff of Asklepios"—known to us by the Latin word *caduceus* (herald-staff). The temples wherein Hippocrates and every healer practiced their care were known as *Asklepieia.* Reflecting the ancient tradition, doctors today take the Hippocratic oath, but on their crest, office, and clothing, they carry the staff of Asklepios with its famous encircling snake. If logical Hippocrates is the Father of Medicine, divine Asklepios is the heralded grandfather.

Who was this Asklepios—was there a real personage behind the myth? What were his healing methods and medicine? To what extent did Hippocrates learn from—or understand—his progenitor? And what do we know about that snake and staff?

We see the staff of Asklepios everywhere: at hospitals, doctors' offices, veterinarians, pharmacies, on medical magazines and ambulances, even the Starship Enterprise. Yet, it is always unexplained, being a symbol so universal that it has become unknown. Medical professionals proudly display the caduceus as a badge of their medical proficiency, but usually cannot tell their patients anything more about it than its name. This complete lack of knowledge needs remedy.

Let's take a look at what a coiled snake, a mythologized healer, and a set of ancient healing practices can tell us about the medicine we are practicing as well as the arts we should be exercising.

The Snake of the Caduceus

What kind of talisman was the snake for the Hellenic forerunners of western civilization? What about the snake mythology appealed to the early philosophers? Did the Hellenes actually use the snakes? What impact and meaning did the snakes carry for our forebearers?

The single snake around Asklepios' staff was the
coluber longissimus, a tree snake
known as *pareiai,* "present,"
and later, also as *phoinix,*
"the resurrected." These
yellow-brown, "friendly"
snakes were known to bask
in the sunlight, hanging peacefully
from trees, as they digested the disease-carrying
rodents they had consumed. The friendly *pareiai* were
associated with the deep rest of contentment.

When they did move, they "were like works of
art", as described by an ancient, unknown voice: "the
elegant movements of the slender body, the shining
brass-colored head—as finely chiseled as the work of
a goldsmith." Pausanias tells us that the *pareiai* were
abundant throughout the Epidaurian Sanctuary and
some were "enormous." He also mentions that a
species, fairer than most, was unique to Epidavros. The
pareiai were a healing tool, their uses ranging from
licking wounds to sleeping with pilgrims.

One of the most celebrated significances of the
snake is the shedding of its skin, which symbolizes a
new beginning and the ever-regenerating life. The
skin-shedding snake was a primary symbol for the
necessary death that precedes spiritual resurrection.
A snake's deathly significance is evinced in its
poisonous bites, and when it swallows its prey whole,
and when it slithers down into the earth. The mortal
implication of being animal-bound has often been

pictured in the snake, whose home is Chthonia, or the Underworld. From the half-snake, half-human Typhon to temptation in Eden, from the tail of the devil to the hair of Medusa, the serpent carries a mortal message—a fear that goes, as Emily Dickenson mused, to "the zero of the bone."

While the snake carried a reminder of death, it also has held mysteries of living knowledge. More primal and significant than the attributes of death and resurrection is the snake's *enlivening* role as a talisman. In the Asklepian tradition, the "friendly" *coluber longissimus* was used for its perceptual impact—visual and feeling—towards full rest.

In our evolutionary heredity, the snake incarnates the bridge between worm and spine, between the dark underworld and the lighted earth. The snake's talismanic force can be discerned in this evolutionary leap to the spine. As spine, the range of energies, high and low, give the living awareness a brighter light and a truer rest than the dim worm. In evolutionary terms, the spine appears dramatically in the snake, and this reptilian backbone ontologically acts as a talisman or deep reminder of the innately ecstatic state accessible via the central nervous system in homo sapiens. More than worm or slug or mere chthonic flesh, the human nervous system uncoils to find energetic highs and lows, esoteric harmonies, and also sentient rest in primal simplicity.

The *columber longissimus* was anciently described as having a "celestial presence" that manifested a healing power. Unlike other snakes, it stood out as "presence*"* and "*phonix*".

Entire volumes could be written on the snake and its use as a fetish and an as an esoteric symbol. For now, let us simply appreciate the snake in its mulitdimensionality—symbolizing and transmitting a deep knowledge of death, resurrection, rest, aliveness, even a celestial vibrance.

The History and Mythology of Asklepios

Asklepios was already the stuff of legends by Homer's time. He was said to have appeared as a living personage in many ages. Genealogical lines of healers can be traced to the name *Asklepiadai,* and we may infer that indeed there was a source personage appearing at the origin of the Western healing tradition. Thessaly claims his birth and folklore tells how his two sons carried his name and healing art south, to Kos and Epidavros. Asklepios and his sons seemed to have been so great in stature that myth, legend, family lines, and history have intermingled, leaving much factual uncertainty. But the reality, greatness, and influence of the

Asklepian healing tradition are beyond doubt. Although we cannot separate myth and history, all the descriptions of the "physician hero" certainly reveal much of the spiritual art of the one or more personages that were called Asklepios.

Even in the myth of his conception, Asklepios was an epiphany: the divine Apollo was his father and the mortal princess Koronis his mother—a natural intermingling of divinity and flesh. But Artemis, Apollo's twin sister, slayed the very pregnant Koronis and placed her body on a pyre, whence Apollo medically removed the infant and saved his love of mortal Koronis.

Asklepios was said to resemble his grandfather, Zeus, in His compassionate mood. Apollo gave his caring son into the care and instruction of the healing centaur, Chiron.

Chiron was the bearer of plant knowledge (*pharmacopia, "spells against death"*) —inherited from far and near: spiritual India, the inspired Middle East, and Africa's Egyptian fount. As "the mythological physician who was the precursor to the luminous physician," Chiron gave his gifts to the world via Asklepios and all healers that followed. But unlike all the other gods, Chiron gave humankind a unique gift: he became wounded, suffered illness, and died. He entered into the Underworld and forever carried the wound, giving caring healers access to the dark, chthonic disturbances and pain of their patients.

As a centaur, Chiron is part animal, part human, and very divine — a three-fold epiphany. He is pictured with a horse's body and a dog for a friend — a human head and torso carrying a power plant and nutritious prey — and his open hand, open face, and upright ears suggest his divinity. Chiron's displayed spectrum of characteristics revealed a wide knowledge: from animal, through the human, to divinity. Or as was said in the mysteries: from dark animal to god-light through *gnosis* (divine knowledge).

This capacity to traverse the planes below the dark earth and urgent animal, and past man into ecstatic Olympia is the meaningful power of the herald, the serpentined staff of Asklepios and the dual-snaked staff of Hermes. The proclamation of the true herald is not about <u>this</u> plane of existence, but about a multitude of realities. The herald-staff, held by a human, stretches from the lower, chthonic underworld to another, open, spiritual, and transcendental domain. Chiron spectrally points to the multidimensional, open-bodied, open-minded, open-hearted revelation that is true health.

From Chiron, Asklepios is said to have learned the herbs, arts and mysteries of healing.

Asklepios was certainly appreciated for his medical knowledge and his *"techne"* (the artful correspondence of pattern and forming). But his healing skills and depth of feeling were given divine superlatives—empowered, it was said, by his legendary caring. Asklepios was not only the "Physician Hero," he was also appreciated as the god of medicine and the divinity of dreams and healing visions. He came to one in dreams when ill, touched one with "divine energy," and regrounded one's faith in regeneration and recovery.

From a religious perspective, the Physician Hero was a priest or channeller of Apollo. Like artists who mystically gave themselves to the Muses in order to recite or dance or play music or to prophesy, the healing priest would avail himself to the visitation of Apollo. Apollo—the divinity who purifies and heals (with his arrows and lyre)—would be supplicated in order to spark again the *physis,* or "blossoming emergence," in those who came infirm (*physis* in Latin is *natura*). The *physis-cians* were the priests who assisted the god to come naturally touch the patient receiver.

From the ancient religious assessment, healing began with an *epiphany*—a touch of the divine energy. This epiphany was the "favor" bestowed by both Apollo and Asklepios. This regenerated spark grew into recovery—a recovery built upon health's very foundation. To rekindle the *physis*, to spark and flare again the feeling of eternal life in the body, was the primary focus in every aspect of the Asklepian healing ceremony.

The Asklepian Healing Ceremony at Epidavros

When the ancient Hellenes wanted to found a new city, they first asked the Oracle at Delphi for Apollo's blessing, then, if the prophecy was positive, received coals from the eternal hearth. Thereupon, they traveled to Epidavros for the sacred snakes, "present, phonix" to take to the new habitat, which were honored as godly presence. It is said that a thousand cities around the Mediterranean began that Apollonian way.

In the ancient world, one did not visit the *Asklepieia* (*Temples of Asklepios*) casually, for it was a sacred occasion. The Asklepian Sanctuary was about the eternal Life that is without ending or beginning: therefore *no one was born there, nor did anyone go there to die.* Only when all the common treatments (such as herbs and rest) had proven insufficient did one approach the *Asklepieia*. Disease was understood to be a disturbance of the *chthonic*, the subterranean and un-conscious (*hades*) energies which needed light. Having understood that healing was participation in *epiphany*, one went to the temple in order to meet the god halfway.

A system of these temples freely served the populace in the healing of disease. The most common donation to the priests and sanctuary was a pig or cock. (Thus we recall Socrates' humorous last words after he drank his "potion" of hemlock, "Krito, we owe Asklepios a cock, pay it and do not neglect it.") *Asklepieia* prospered on the gratitude of the people they had served. The central temple of this religious network was at Epidavros (L. Epidauros), praised for centuries for its miraculous healings.

If you came ill to Epidavros in its 5th-4th century BCE peak, you you would marvel at the entrance to the santuary: the majestic *Propylaea*, its 57-foot arch supported by two rows of marble columns—six petaled Corinthian columns on the inside and six simple Ionian columns on the elegant outside. You would hear the singing of the priestesses welcoming you to the blessed ground, chanting and intoning, "May the healing divinity never leave us!"

Of the three main mystery temples (Eleusian, Delphic, and Epidaurian), this one was the most devoted to Beauty. Visitors would be awe-struck by its harmonious art and by the care that had been taken to achieve such divine perfection and balance. Beauty and blessings overwhelmed the inner being. Beauty—in marble, in paintings, and song—was the first of the blessings that would train the pilgrims' attention to rest in the divine. Through beauty and trust, true healing would begin. Beauty and the good, in Plato's report, were the acknowledged means to bring harmony and health to each one.

To attend to the sacred nature of existence, the patient-supplicant was served at every turn. Majestic art, heritage groves and a host of waters, wise theatre and wise counsel, medical potions and developed skills, priests of power and "temple sleep" all bathed the infirm with healing force and with "admirable divine power."

This power certainly had a lasting effect. Almost two millennia later, Henry Miller wrote, "At Epidauros, in the stillness, in the great peace that came over me, I heard the heart of the world beat....There is no mystery in my mind as to the nature of the cures which were wrought at this great therapeutic centre of the ancient world. Here the healer himself was healed, the first and most important step in the development of the art, which is not medical but religious."

Inscribed over the majestic archway were the rhythmed words:

ΑΓΝΟΝ ΞΡΗ ΝΗΟΙΟΣ ΘΗΟΔΕΟΣ ΕΝΤΟΣ ΙΟΝΤΑ
ΕΜΜΕΝΙΑ ΑΓΝΕΙΗ Δ ΕΣΤΙ ΦΡΟΝΕΙΝ ΟΣΙΑ

PURE MUST BE HE WHO ENTERS
THE FRAGRANT TEMPLE
PURITY MEANS TO THINK NOTHING
BUT HOLY THOUGHTS

Once the grand archway had been transversed, one entered into the home of a god. Steles, taller than a man, marked the way inside the

Sanctuary with tales of miracles. The first began with the inscription:

ΘΕΟΣ ΤΩΥΑ ΑΓΑΘΑ

GOD! GOOD FORTUNE!

Then followed the "Cures of Apollo and Asklepios," with abundant stories of health and gratitude. These "Tablets of miracles" and human testimonies transmitted infectious faith to the pilgrims. Throughout the Sanctuary—on tablets, walls, and in scrolls in the extensive library—

miracles were attributed to the "admirable divine power." The library also held a thorough collection of all the great works of the culture, and the supplicant was heartily encouraged to spend many hours soaking up the light of inspired or mused writings.

Inside the sanctuary, the nearby hills caressed the holy ground as "the crade of medicine". Across the landscaped cove and templed fields, one could see in the distance a perfect amphitheater, carved into the hill. This acoustically flawless crucible held 14,400 participants in intimate instruction and is still used to this day.

    Pausanias, a second-century traveler, visited Epidauros in 160 C.E., while it was still prospering (though by then some of its best art had been plundered). He reported: "The sacred grove of Asklepios is surrounded by bounds on every side. No men die or women give birth within the enclosure; the same rule is observed on the island of Delos [Birthplace of Apollo].

    "Tablets stood within the enclosure. Of old there were more of them; in my time six were left. On these tablets are engraved the names of men and women who were healed by Asklepios: together with the disease from which each suffered and how he was cured. Apart from the others, stands an ancient tablet which says that Hippolytos dedicated 20 horses to the god." Three tablets survived in good shape and can be seen in the present-day museum at the sanctuary.

Asklepios' daughter, Hygeia (lit. "Health"), was given a position high with her father—as cleanliness was understood to be a necessary foundation to health. Pilgrims were surrounded with extreme hygiene, beauty, and wise counsel. They were given bedding and nourishment and time to adapt to the religious disposition of the sacred environment. They were encouraged to release their conventional roles and their concerned or clever mind by wandering in the good company of splendorous groves, friendly, exquisite gardens, beautiful snakes, masterpieces of art, inspired stories, gifted physicians and lively priests.

Pilgrims were treated to rest and sustenance, and served by the healthy properties and devotional ambiance of the sacred ground. By day, continuous songs, chants, and music mingled with nature's sounds to envelop the pilgrims in aural resonances and praiseful tones. Other healing tools abounded: an abundance of fountains and mineral baths (for the water's intimacy with the chthonic underworld), harmonic athletics, therapeutic touch, massage, purgatives, and *pharmacopia* teas and potions.

When the pilgrim had received sufficient preparation and purification, the high priests of

Asklepios met with them, so that the infirm might gain sufficient self-understanding to appreciate the ways in which they might be contributing to their disease process. This insight-sharing by the priests to the pilgrims was known as *Nootherapia* (usually translated as *mind-healing*). The therapy usually began by focusing on the dreams of the patient. Insight was understood to be Apollo's arrows—for the *Asklepiades* originated the great homeopathic saw, "The wounder heals."

The discussed dreams and the patients' relation to their own subconscious ephemera gave the trained priests an avenue into the "wrong thinking" of the ill. On the basis of this Apollonian penetration, the priest guided the ill to grow in self-understanding—then suggested a right orientation. This *Nootherapeia* always included a saying from the archway: *Phronein Ousia,* "Give your attention to the Presence."

The presence and counsel of the high priests blessed the patient to feel and breathe deeply the faith and felt connection to the divine power. This harmony was understood to be Apollo's lyre, and by this harmony, the pilgrim began to let loose the unconscious clutching at sorrows and cacophonic unease. Gratitude began to lighten the soul again.

By the good company, lyric wisdom, and radiance of the priests, the patients observed the falsity of their own concerned and weak disposition—and when the pilgrim was given such a realistic eye, they were led to intuit the "natural state of harmony." Gaining strength (*Eros*) in this natural harmonious awareness (*Nous*), one understood the self-created disease metaphorically as a dreamy chimera—a fanciful monster with a lion's head, a goat's body and a serpent's tail. Upon seeing the unreality that supported the disease, the pilgrim began to turn to the divine healing power. Asklepios was thus known as *Asklepios Nootherapia, The God of Mind-Healing.* They called this realistic change of disposition, *"metanoia"* (meta—above + nous—luminous awareness, or *the higher awareness).* This deep conversion from the unreal to what is most real gave the Asklepian healing ceremony uncommon depth.

Once the patient had been graced with *metanoia,* the lay *Asklepides,* the lay physicians, would administer to them a variety of what we call medicine: from *pharmakopia* to surgeries. But it was explicited noted that without *metanoia,* the lay *Asklepiades* could only administer temporary relief from illness.

Plato clearly admired the medical art and science of the Asklepian ceremony. In the *Symposium,* he speaks through the physician-philosopher Eryximachos: "Medicine must, indeed, be able to make the most hostile elements in the body friendly and loving towards each other. It was by knowing the means by which to introduce 'Eros' and harmony in these that, as the poets here say and I also believe, our forefather Asklepios established this art-science of ours."

Hubris and Medusa

The other theme the priests instructed the patient about was true beauty—and its counterfeit, *hubris*, or self-fascinated arrogance. In the sensitivity to *hubris*, the patient was subject to Apollo's insightful arrows. Self-understanding further allowed the process of grace, or reliance on what is greater than human virtues. By this divine help, the patient-pilgrim would see beyond human self-concerns and passing concerns, where the immortal beatific is coincident with the source of life. This revelation was refreshed for the supplicant by the study of Medusa.

Medusa (lit. *ruler* or *queen*) was of such beauty that she claimed rivalry with Aphrodite. The arrogant teen Medusa even made love to Poseidon in a temple dedicated to the virgin Athena. However, Medusa's arrogance and self-fascination brought her a perfect curse: she appeared hideous, with serpentined hair, boar's tusks, a terrible grin, snub nose, and staring eyes. Flesh-bound men would to turn to stone when they merely gazed upon her surface appearance.

Athena, the virgin goddess of craft, skill, and war gave Perseus her breast-plate (*aegis*) and shield, and challenged him to cut off Medusa's head. Using a cap of invisibility from the nymphs, and winged shoes and a sword from Hermes, Perseus used the shine in Athena's bronze shield to see Medusa without gazing at her.

Hermes' sword was described as *"adamant,"* indicating the insistence required to cut through superficial appearances. Using the cutting power of free Hermes, Perseus was able to *adamantly* slice off Medusa's head (and put it in a pouch the nymphs also thoughtfully provided). From the wound and spouted blood of her decapitation, the winged horse Pegasus was born, announcing in flight the heartful freedom that comes when surface beauty is seen beyond. This blood was also gathered by Asklepios, as it held the heart-power set free by adamant discrimination. (And such it was that the image of Medusa's severed head appeared on Athena's aegis.)

The priests also counseled the supplicants on matters such as diet, posture, purification, fasting, the art of breath, and invoking the powers of their divinities. By the time of Hippocrates, the healers even performed effective surgeries. But always, in every Asklepian time, the primacy of the healing was grounded in a new self-understanding, a new responsibility, and renewed faith in the true Beauty of existence. Herbs, drugs, and surgery were certainly appreciated, but most central to health was "right thinking." This changed disposition was served by dream reflections, by considering the chimeric nature of disease, and the heart of real beauty.

Such it was that within the sacred ground of the *Asklepieion* at Epidavros was an entire mini-sanctuary devoted to Aphrodite. After counseling, the patient was directed to contemplate true beauty there.

The Greatest Theatre

When the body became balanced and rested, one was served with the healing art of the greatest theatre in all the land—a xplace of humor, wisdom and *perfect harmonics*. Dedicated performers and sage wisdom brought the play's lessons to the viewers with such intimacy that the separation between self and play dissolved. This was particularly true of the 35 dramas of Epicharmos. Although none have survived, we know from his contemporaries that these plays were held in the very highest esteem for the profundity of their philosophical and metaphysical ideas. Indeed, Diogenes Laertis tells us that Plato kept the works of Epicharmos under his pillow! Listen again to Epicharmos' call to consciousness at Epidavros: "It is the *Nous* that sees and hears, the rest is deaf and blind."

Pausanias relates of that theatre: "In the Epidaurian sanctuary there is a theatre in my opinion

most especially worth seeing ... and for harmony and beauty what architect could vie with Polycleitos? For it was Polycleitos who made this theatre and the round building also. Within the grove is a temple of Artemis and an image of Epione [Asklepios' wife]; also a sanctuary of Aphrodite and Themis; and a Stadion formed like most Greek stadions, by bands of earth; also a fountain worth seeing for its roof and general splendor."

The priests and assistants kept track of the development of the pilgrims' strength and how each responded to the "preparations." They decided who was already healed and could leave, who would continue the preparations of counsel, rest, teas, and the like, and also who was needed the final epiphany in the *Tholos* and "Enkoimisis," the Temple Sleep of the *Abaton*.

The Inner Sanctum

Throughout the inner sanctum was a plethora of Apollo's snakes, considered to be manifestations of the healing divinity. Dominating the holiest of sacred grounds were the Temple of Asklepios, the round and magnificent *Tholos,* later known as the *rotunda,* and the *Abaton,* or place where the initiated slept and received the supreme healing *epiphany.*

The Temple of Asklepios is patterned after the Temple of Zeus at Olympia. Like the Olympian Temple, it also faced east and stood its ground in Doric order—80 feet long by 44 feet wide, its outer columns 17 feet high. Its tufa walls were painted white, with multicolored capitals and ornaments. The roof was of cypress and pine and covered with tiles. Winged Nikes (Victories) adorned the pediment as did Centaurs and Amazons. The floor was black Eleusian marble, and the approach was marked with black and white tiles. The inside walls were filled with artistic masterpieces depicting the lessons of Asklepios and his relations.

Unlike all other Temples in Hellas—which swung their doors wide only on celebrations—the Temple of Asklepios was opened daily, during the lighted hours. From sunrise to sunset, every day for hundreds of years, songs and chants filled the sacred space. The daily ceremony at Epidavros began just before sunrise at the Temple of Asklepios when the

priestesses cried out "Lord Paieon!" in invocation to the god of healing.

As the day broke, the epiphany was signalled by sacrificing a rooster and opening of the doors on Asklepios' Temple so that the dawn sunlight illuminated the god in the Temple. The women sang aloud, "It is day, the temple door is open, the curtain is drawn." Supplicants followed the priests and priestesses into the holy habitat and joyfully joined in many cycles of hymn (Awaken! Awaken Asklepios! Awaken pilgrims! Awaken and hear thy hymn!"). Unfortunately, the famous paean of Sophocles, which for centuries was sung in the *Asklepieia*, is lost.

There is no doubt, however, that the Homeric Hymn to Asklepios was chanted there:

To the healer of sicknesses, Asklepios, I sing!
In the Deotian plain of Argos, goddess-like Koronis,
daughter of King Phlegyras, bore him,
a great joy to mortals, a soother of chthonic pains.
Hail to you, lord; I pray to you with my song.

The repetitive hymnals served to focus the mind, emotions, and body. At first, one relaxed and enjoyed the resonance of sound, body, melody, heart, meaning, space, sacred Temple, and then joined in the singing. All the while, one's eyes would feast on the magnificent statue of Asklepios, three and a half times life-size. Pausanias: "The god is seated on a throne, grasping a staff, while holding his other hand over the head of the serpent; and a dog, lying by his side, is also re-presented. Beside the throne in relief are the deeds of Argive heroes: of Bellerophon against the Chimera, and Perseus cutting off Medusa's head."

Like the Olympian Zeus and the Athena on the Acropolis, the Asklepios of Epidavros was "chryselephantine," meaning all the flesh of Asklepios was represented in ivory and all the clothing in richly jeweled gold. To gaze upon such beauty and care in the shimmering dawning sunlight, while immersed in heart-song, was to see a god. He was called *Soter*, the Saviour, as the priests cried out, "The god behold! Behold the god! Bow down to the Saviour in word and spirit, all who stand here! That we may see his beauty as our blessing, Here at this shrine!"

Asklepios sat on his throne with his staff and snake and dog. At his side, also in chryselephantine, was the Chimera, pointing to the illusion of the suffering dream, and the other side is the adamant Perseus and the severed head of Medusa, who confused Beauty with her egoic self.

For those stubborn cases whose dis-ease persisted, there was the *Tholos*, the *rotunda*, called also *Thymele, altar,* and *Incubatio.* Built by Polycleitos the Younger, who also designed the auditorily perfect theatre, the *Thymele* was considered to rank with the most perfect and gracious monuments in all the world.

Round in form, seventy-two feet across, the Tholos was surrounded externally by a colonnade of 26 Doric columns. Behind the columns was the circular wall, decorated with the extraordinary paintings of the famous Pausias. Pausanias described two of them: one was a divine child (presumed by Pausanias to be Eros, but more likely Apollo) picking up his lyre, having discarded his bow and arrows, and a female bacchant (presumed by Pausanias to be *Methe, Drunkenness*), drinking out of a crystal goblet.

Moving inward across the black and white marble floor, we come to another circle of fourteen marble columns, capped in elaborate Corinthian flourish. The ceiling coffered the inner cylinder and was magnificently painted.

What went on here? No one really knows. We know the epiphany received here was considered the deepest, reserved for the most needful. Records reveal that the chosen pilgrims came to this *Thymele* before being taken to the *Abaton* temple to sleep. Today, we can still see how the Tholos sat upon a labyrinthian foundation, with pathways to the *Abaton* beside it. We can assume the labyrinths and pathways were expressly built for Apollo's snakes. And while snakes were in evidence here, archeology has yet to uncover a detailed description of the ceremonial or religious use of the "Altar."

Realizing Polycleitos designed it, we must assume its harmonics were perfect and so a therapy of sound would have been employed here. It is not hard to imagine an ill pilgrim, lying on the altar, surrounded by the tones and humming of the Temple priests and priestesses, and, while relaxing into the vibrance, receiving the potent therapeutic touch of a spirit-filled healer.

This entire incantation was also pervaded by the "friendly" *pareiai* —as the Temple was the core nexus of "Apollo's presence."

The human contact, care, and invocation were not engaged for mere comfort, but transmitted "tangible divine power"— which washed even the subconscious limitations still presumed by the patient. The touch of the god and the epiphany of divine infusion flooded the pilgrim entirely.

Temple Sleep

After the epiphany in the round *Thymele*, the "initiated" were taken next door to the *Abaton* for the "final stage of *enkoimisis*," *Temple Sleep*. It was said that babies and young children naturally enjoy this "temple sleep." It is the deep awareness that one is abundantly cared for, that the substance and condition of real life is utterly benevolent, that truly one is floating is a sea of graciousness and beauty, continually baptized in providence. Lay thy head upon This pillow.

Temple sleep is the deepest rest, perfect stillness "like an animal in its lair", connecting us to that heart-deep and spiritual power that is always and already our real situation. Radiant health is the natural condition we hide with our habitual concern. Temple sleep's depth washes all concern and unease into a transfiguring faith and Apollonian, radiant health. Temple sleep empowered the pilgrim to be relaxed utterly, releasing all unease and disease to the divine care. This cleansing was evidenced by the visitation of the god (Apollo or Asklepios) in that evening's dreams, signalling that the healing was taking place, most deeply.

Emerging in dreams, a feeling and perhaps a vision of the god tells you that you have been touched and that your healing had occurred. Consider the words from the dream of a Roman general, who reports that Apollo/Asklepios came to him and said,

Be not afraid; I shall come [with you to Rome]
and leave my statues,
But see this serpent, as it twines around
The rod I carry: mark it well, and learn it,
For I shall be this serpent, only larger,
Like a celestial presence.

From deep and primal simplicity, a deep and primal energy is awakened. Temple sleep, *enkoimisis*, the deepest, primal rest, releases the un-ease and chthonic disturbances of the patient into blessedness, and the body—via the breath—drinks blissfully, undoing the un-ease and dis-ease.

This deep relaxation were served more than by the purgative, psychosomatic, and psychological aids. Temple sleep was explicitly empowered by the dual talismanic force of the *pareiai*, Apollo's "present" snakes. Their presence served to bring the patient to fully rest and from that stillness to, radiate and animate the power of life in the body. Temple sleep cleaned and embraced the grateful with overwhelming, sweet force. *Enkoimisis* was to sleep in the arms of the divine beloved.

This final epiphany was experienced as "the flaring-up of a divine child ... just like at Eleusis." In Aristophanes' *Plutus*, Plutos, the blind god of riches, opened his eyes at the Asklepieion, and sang (via the chorus), "To him I cry, the beautiful and great light of man, Asklepios."

The Death of Asklepios

The myth of Asklepios' death also contained a profound lesson. When Hippolytus, the leader of the Amazons, died, Artemis, the virginal goddess of female discretion, appealed to Asklepios to restore her devotee to life. The Hero Physician was so adept at conducting the life-force that he succeeded in the task, and Hippolytus was resurrected. As was noted on a tablet at the entrance to the Sanctuary, Hippolytus immediately gave 20 horses to the *Asklepieia*. Hades mightily complained to Zeus that Asklepios was upending the divine order. Zeus agreed, picked up one of His thunderbolts and hurled it to earth where Asklepios stood.

This method of death (*enelysios*—one struck by lightning) was most prized in the ancient world. Zeus Himself decreed it, so all clinging to life could be released. Thereby struck by Zeus, one did not tour the Underworld after death, did not choose between the waters of forgetfulness or remembrance, was not judged, but passed directly to the paradise of *Elysium* (an etymological derivative of *enelysion,* a place made sacred by lightning strikes). Even though Asklepios himself arrogantly forgot the divine law, his punishment was gracious. He completed his life and caused a sanctuary with his death.

What lessons were gained from Asklepios' death? Certainly that the divine order is not to be violated, but this could be said of all transgressions. Religiously, it could be said that one's practice is to cling to the ways of life and not to the ways of death. But even this law can be idealized, that one should cling to life at all costs. In the midst of disease or unease in one's present form, it is true, one should cling to the "eternal" life that is naturally felt in health and intuited in happiness.

But death is a uncompromising message in this mortal realm, and one cannot absolutely cling to the passing forms of life without inevitable and unnecessary suffering.

The word in the Christian scripture that means eterenal life is *zoe*, not *bios*. When the Master from Galilee explained his gift of eternal life, he was not promising an angel-like version of yourself forever. Living (as if) in the personal company of the person of love, you gracefully inherit real reality, the domain of *zoe*, eternal life everywhere.

This discretion between the eternal life (*zoe*) and the passing forms of life (*bios*) is a lightning-insight of Zeus. It reveals the difference between the sacred and the precious. Our *biological* lives are to be cherished, yes, but more than clinging preciousness, life is sacredly free. Life is to be held and beholden, not arrogantly claimed nor preciously clutched. The death of Asklepios is a signal that clinging to life is not an absolute, and even the mortally precious must be

sanctified by being given up to the greater life that
sustains and heals us and the world in natural radiance.

Orpheus, the Katha Upanishad, and the Secret Way Beyond Death

PURE FRIENDS!
SONS AND DAUGHTERS OF THE EARTH AND
STARRY SKY!
ESCAPE FROM THE SPINDLE OF NECESSITY AND
THE SORROWFUL, WEARY ROUND UPON THE
WHEEL OF BIRTH.
ENTER THE WREATH OF HEAVEN
FROM MORTALS BECOME GODS

LOOK UP FROM THE POOL OF LETHE
TO THE WHITE POPLAR TREE.
LISTEN TO THE COUNSEL OF
THE JUDGE OF THE DEAD
TURN TO THE REFRESHING
WATERS OF REMEMBRANCE.
RELIGIOUSLY PRACTICE REMEMBRANCE.

COMING FROM THE PURE
DRINK IMMORTAL AMBROSIA
QUENCHING EVERY THIRST
BY THE GRACE OF
THE RELEASING DIVINITIES.
RISE WITH WINGED ENJOYMENT
TO THE PRIVILEGED FIELDS OF ELYSIUM
WHERE BLESSED COMPANY AWAITS.
O HAPPY AND BLESSED ONE,
THOU SHALT BE GOD INSTEAD OF MORTAL.

INITIATES! FOLLOW THE DIVINE!
DISCIPLINE THE PRISON BODY!
BALANCE! PURIFY!
ABSTAIN FROM EATING ANYTHING
THAT BREATHES LIKE YOU DO.
LIVE A PURIFYING AND TEMPERATE LIFE
DEVOTED TO THE UNLIMITED.

FOLLOW THE GOD
AND MOVE FROM CLOSED TO OPEN EYES.
AWAKEN TO THE ISLAND OF THE BLEST!
BEHOLD THE FLOWERS OF GOLDEN BLAZING,
AND ON THE SHORE, RADIANT TREES,
WITH INTERTWINING RISING HANDS
CROWNING THE ECSTASY, OPEN EYES

DRINK AGAIN
THE WATERS OF REMEMBRANCE
IN GOOD COMPANY, PRACTICE REMEMBRANCE.

LIKE A KID WHO HAS FALLEN INTO MILK
TRUE SATISFACTION   DIVINE DISTRACTION
ENTHUSIASTIC PROPHETS
WITH THE DIVINE VISION
OPEN ONLY TO THE SOUL IN GOD
INSPIRED, FILLED WITH GOD
THE UNBROKEN RADIANCE OF DIVINITY

—sample collection of Orphic saws

Lib. 10.   ORPHEVS CYTHARA FERAS ET INANIMA TRAHIT.

Orpheus dulcisonâ dum carmina voce sususrat
Fixa sono stabant bestia, saltus, avis.

Def: Orpheus süsse Harffenklang,
Sinn, und leblose ding bezwang.

Orpheus, the Katha Upanishad, and the Secret Way Beyond Death

Orpheus or parts of Orphism are mentioned directly or implicitly in almost every major drama, philosophical treatise or theological rhapsody of the ancient Hellenes. The teachings ascribed to "Orpheus" were so thoroughly widespread in the ancient Hellenic world — especially in the formative pre-Socratic era — that Orphism could be said to be the spiritual background of the Hellenic miracle. To understand the spiritual foundation of *logos* and the religious and spiritual origins of Western logic, we must understand the *theo-logos* of Orpheus.

If asked to give a summary of "Orphism," most would be taxed — all but the classicists, and even their answer would be "academic" in its portrayal. Yet, if we look carefully, and with a heightened spiritual sense, we can see that the tenets and teachings of Orphism merged into the very fabric of the Western mind — *and by such interwoven familiarity has become essentially forgotten.*

It behooves us to transcend our blindness of familiarity and look with fresh eyes upon Orphism, not as a scholarly investigation and speculation—that has been done, but to behold a complex religion of wondrous force and reinherit the spiritual awe beyond thinking. "True philosophy begins in wonder" indeed.

We need only to look at Plato to see the pervasive effect of "Orpheus" upon Western civilization. And if Western philosophy is the footnotes of Plato (as proposed by Alfred North Whitehead), it could also be said that Socrates and the pre-Socratics are the bibliography. The literature and lessons of Orpheus, the *Orphika,* compose the West's inspirational source text for Orphism.

We have nothing directly from the *Orphika*, save the quotes of others. In fact, Plato was said to be able to quote line after line from the legendary *Orphika* — usually on matters of the immortality of the "soul". Speaking as a Westerner, our conception of our very souls is Socratic-Platonic, and therefore imbued with "Orpheus." With his very life, Socrates gave the Orphic soul its modern incarnation.

In the *Phaedo*, Plato-Socrates honors Orphism in the very highest regards and twice equates the soul of "true philosopher" with that of the realisers of the Orphic mysteries. "For the initiated are in my opinion none other than those who have been true philosophers." On his last day alive (according to Plato), Socrates did not speak of politics or Forms above forms, or even the kinds of love, but appropriately was full of "the ancient teachings" about the Underworld Orphic tour that the soul navigates after death.

Fortunately, we have an abundance of fragments about "Orpheus" and Orphism. Unfortunately, they are scattered along a millennia, from before and after the records of numbered time. In fact, the fragments are so scattered, old, and suspect, we cannot even "prove" that Orpheus himself ever existed. Indeed, the "evidence" is twofold that he was and wasn't an actual historical person.

In fact, it has been debated for <u>millennia</u> whether Orpheus an historical person, a figure of legend, or a collection of stories. Certainly, he could be all of those things. The physician, historian, and scholar Apollodorus Askelpidae (d. ~120 BCE) bluntly stated that Orpheus "invented the mysteries of Dionysus."

On the other hand, many (including Aristotle, over three hundred years after the time of "the Master") claimed that Orpheus was a mythic creation from the "Rhapsodies" of Onomakritos —the court seer and revered "Orphic Initiator" for the ruler of Athens, Peisistratos (from 561-527 BCE). Others have attributed the twenty-four sheets of pure gold (the *lamellae)* inscribed with Orphic scripture to Pythagoras. The debate on Orpheus has gone on for twenty-four centuries and his corporeality has never been a scholarly certainty.

While scholarly propositions on the reality of Orpheus often look for historical evidence and then reports on found facts, the debate fails to account for the deeply-moving meanings of the found material itself. Therefore, instead of again surveying the body of Orphic literature, or touring the landscape of scholarly opinion, let us focus on the teaching itself, the sacred words, and therein consider if we find simply stories, myth, and a primitive religion — or a deeper, penetrating, and moving understanding. Indeed, it is my contention that finding such penetrating revelation would be the clearest evidence that Orpheus was the name of a real human — for only "prophet's words" could inspire the Hellenes with such transformative force.

Therefore, let us proceed as theological, forensic scientists and reconstruct the complexion and face of Orpheus from the metaphorical skeleton, and, as we shall see, the "singing head" of Orphism that we do possess.

Probably the most thorough work on Orpheus was done by W.K.C. Guthrie, who came down squarely on the side that assumes at least one great mystic took on the legendary name of "Orpheus." But as he points out, the naysayers make good points as well, and the misty, pre-historical time is no place to argue facts. Contradictions exist: for instance, "Orpheus" predates Homer as he is mentioned in the Iliad (~725 BCE), yet Orpheus' theological teaching would have to post-date Hesiod ~710 BCE (as we shall see later). Paradoxically, to bridge the gaps in the "evidence," Orpheus needs to be both an historical person with a legend and a demi-god with a myth.

In the eighth century before the Common Era, Hellas adopted the alphabet from the Phoenicians, but added letters for vowels. Hellas not only reachieved literacy, she invigorated literary expression, — as evidenced by Homer and Hesiod. With literacy restored, there began a period of what has been called the "orientalization of Hellas". Babylonian Zorastrianism, Levant Monism, as well as Brahmanic Upanishads can be seen infusing Hellas with their finest words.

Herodotus reported that in this early literate period, Orpheus "hailed from Thrace, the greatest nation on earth, outside of India." Thrace was well-known for its cosmopolitan position at the far western end of the great caravan roads that led east to India, where wise men were exposed to the Vedanta of the Upanishads (800–400 B.C.E.). While records cannot be substantiated with weak facts, it is not difficult to see how some Thracian "prophet" or god-possessed priest took on the mystic name "Orpheus" as he enjoyed the spiritual teachings from "the spiral origin, the seat of the world," Upanishadic India.

In fact, the similarities and transparencies of the Katha Upanishad and the teachings of Orpheus are striking: both were grounded in conversations with the Lord of Death; both speak of austerities and acetic purification (*katharsis*); both harp upon the immortal soul beyond birth and death; both speak of discriminating between semblance, binding illusion, and liberating Truth. Both the Upanishads and Orphism call the listener to renounce the false and choose the Real, and by this conversion, both speak of inheriting "eternal," "perfect ecstasy."

It is no affectation that the Orphics referred to one another as "*Katharoi*," usually translated as "Pure." More meaning can be harvested as we note that "*Katharoi*" alluded to the purifying *katharsis* that was the necessary foundation to a divine life; the *kathartic* message is clear: spiritual work was first a purifying preparation. *Kata* or "down" is the root of *katharsis*, indicating one has gone down and returned, purified.

And "Katha" is the name of the sage who wrote the Katha Upanishad and founded the Kathaka school belonging to the Yajur-Veda. His name, like the word *katharsis*, has etymological roots which translate as "purification." To study "Pure Orpheus" and Orphism, we must review the Katha Upanishad, drink from the same stream as Orpheus.

> "*The Hereafter never reveals itself to a person devoid of discrimination, heedless, and perplexed by the delusion of wealth. 'This world alone exists,' he thinks, 'and there is no other.' Again and again he comes under my sway,*" says Yama, the Lord of Death.
>
> —Katha Upanishad I.ii.6

Prior to the Upanishads, mythology and shamanism were the extent of religious knowledge and experience. As the myth-laden Vedas evolved into the discriminative Upanishads, the shamanistic, body-based urge for free-feeling was satisfied and completed in the rare air of mystic and sage realization. With deep equanimity and native joy, one may drink the ambrosial, unchanging consciousness that witnesses all changes, all transformations, all states—waking, dreaming, sleeping, and dying. That sage understanding was introduced into the West with Orphism.

Up until the Upanishadic Orpheus, the shamanistic rites of the West were best known through the intoxicated ravings of mystic Dionysus. These celebrations served to resurrect, enliven, and illumine the spirit of the celebraters, the bacchants. With the advent of "Lord Orpheus," sage consciousness "enlightened" those Dionysian mysteries with Apollonian penetration and harmony. Apollo himself was said to have come to the Hellenes through Thrace from the Vedic northeast.

As the reappearance of literacy was congealing the bardic legends, the "oriental" Dionysian religious practice of intense celebration, *orgia*, spread like wildfire across the Balkan peninsula. For the ancient Hellenes, the orgiastic teachings and shamanistic rites promised a spiritual release through raving celebration, or *bacchos ecstasy*.

These Dionysian celebrations served to resurrect, enliven, and illumine the spirit of the *bacchants*, the "ravers". For the participants, the Dionysian celebratory rites served to transform all that was subjectively dark into ecstasy—or, to borrow a phrase from Blake, Dionysus indicated "the path of excess that led to the palace of wisdom."

However, in response to the excesses of Dionysus, another voice emerged in the seventh century, the Apollonian song of Orpheus. With the advent of "Lord Orpheus," mystic consciousness enlightened those shamanistic mysteries with Apollonian penetration and harmony. This transformation was universally acknowledged throughout the ancient world, so that by the sixth century, the poet Ibykos referred to the Master of the mysteries as "famous Orpheus".

Orpheus was "the realizer of Dionysus" <u>and</u> "Priest of Apollo," triumphantly acknowledged as the one who tamed, measured, and revealed the meaning of the intoxicating rituals. He was called "Lord (or) Master of the Mysteries" for over a thousand years, and was also known as "the Prophet who enlightened the raving rites."

"Clothed in radiance," the legendary "Lord Orpheus" brought Apollonian stillness, temperance, and restraint to the sensual shamanic. As the Western hymnist of Upanishadic realization, Orpheus represented the sage completion and transcendence of mystic shamanism in ancient Hellas. Restrained, yet unsuppressed, free within the limits of harmony,

Orphism balanced pleasure and wisdom, body and soul, outgoing and inward energies, joy and transcendence.

> *"When the five instruments of knowledge stand still, together with the mind, and when the intellect does not move, that is called the Supreme State. This, the firm control of the senses, is what is called yoga."*
> — Katha Upanishad II.ii.10

For the Orphic practitioner, this enlargement of conscious joy began with a cleansing of the body, followed by a deeply expressed communion, which in turn matured into ecstatic self-realization. This three-staged way of explicit purification, sacred communion, and "constant ecstasy" expressed itself in invocations, in rhapsodic, sacred hymns and wise teachings, in the noble call to limit-transcendence, and by the mysteries and divine presence of the source person: "Reformer and Prophet" Orpheus—then through the lineage of his initiates. This lineage of theology bridging between mythological poesy and prosaic philosophy became Western thought. As Walter Wili so clearly stated in 1944, "The Mysteries are then the common line between the Paleolithic shaman and the tragedian of the classic age."

Purification and Remembrance

Unabashedly Western, the Orphics used the natural harmony found in pleasure as the first sign of the transcendental harmony. Dionysian sensual dance and intoxicants, the music of the flute, lyre, drums, and the incantations, recitations, and poetry of the *theologoi* (those Orphics attending to *theos logos*) all combined to guide the feeling, breathing *psyche* toward the joy that is unlimited.

Released in joyous ecstasy, the immortal nature of the soul flashed forward and the initiate thus inspired began the great transformation to a life divine. It is interesting to note that ecstasy was considered <u>the</u> evidence that the flesh may intercourse with the divine.

The substance of the Orphic life was to prepare the soul for sustained ecstasy, to live a life signed not by the usual destiny of ordinary self-fulfilling *pathos* but by balanced, self-transcending divinity (*apathos*). This *katharsis* had many implications in behavior and prescription; the most mentioned was vegetarianism and general nonviolence. "He taught men to abstain from killing."

Many Orphic precepts prescribed the spiritual necessity of engaging the balanced, moral life as the cleansing foundation of sustained religious embrace.

This balancing life consisted of vowing to a life of moral actions, dietary restraints, study, meditation, and purifications (such as fasting and breathing techniques). It is interesting to note that Orphics ritually daubed their skin with wet clay and let it dry to absorb impurities (and were known for great skin?). Another earthly (and meditative) ritual is seen in the

Orphic practice of being buried up to the neck in the mother earth—serving not only the purification of the body, but also requiring strength in "utter stillness," *hesychia* (ee-see-hee-ah).

Thereupon balanced, cleansed, and stilled by the way of Orpheus, every intoxicating ritual of Dionysus was an occasion to release feeling and behold the divine foundation of real existence. It was noted that only those who were well-cleansed could sustain the embrace of ecstasy. For those dedicated disciples, the mysteries of divine communion (*koinonia*) and divine knowledge (*gnosis*) grew as an immortal and moral soul.

By growing in communion and *gnosis*, immortality came to those who had been imprisoned as passing breathers. (*Psychein,* "to breathe", is the root of *"psyche".*) Sustaining communion via the breath is a universal practice, and it can provide a soulful link to the undisturbed and joyous awareness beyond waking, dreaming, sleeping, and death.

The immortal psyche or deep spirit that became evident in growing balance and purity resonated in harmony to the ambrosial awareness found as the self-radiant, numinous essence of everything. The *harmonia* of the *kosmos* overwhelmed the inner being and the soul found itself already within "the unbroken light of divinity".

> *Having realized Atman, which is soundless, intangible, formless, undecaying, and likewise tasteless, eternal, and odorless,*

having realized That which is without beginning and end, beyond the Great, and unchanging—one is freed from the jaws of death.
—Katha Upanishad I.iii.15

For centuries in the ancient world, the phrase "according to him" referred to Orpheus, and, according to him, when one becomes cleansed by the purification work and divinity invades the body, the seat of right thinking is found in the diaphragm and full breath. Deeply breathing, the soul finds itself already rising and eternally resting in the royal Fields of Elysium. This enlightened joy began (in words ascribed to Orpheus) "the years of pleasure."

The Transforming Soul of Orpheus

Even though Orpheus was legendary for his vibrant conduction of mystical divine power to those in his presence, this loving, direct experiential effect he had on people is often overlooked or dismissed. Speech about sacred company is easily misunderstood — especially in the West. This is partly due to the ineffable nature of all such experiences (which are therefore described in "mythological" metaphors), and partly due to the fact that the very notion is unknown to most Westerners, incongruent with our world view of insistent independence — and therefore spiritual transmission, while extremely rare, is generally simply rejected, neither believed nor understood.

The capacity of Orpheus to "transmit the feeling of communion" was heralded and noted as being most unique, what set him apart from other holy men. And his lineage of initiated transmitters went forward, spreading his teaching as they demonstrated it in remembrance of him.

In the case of Orpheus, it was mythically reported that his lyre's heart-force exceeded all animal and siren calls—and was reported to have even calmed the waters of a troubled sea. Like the Buddha touching the earth and transforming this world into the divine domain, Orpheus transmitted a lyric joy stronger than death itself.

Even prior to Orpheus, *athanatos (immortality),* was *the* epithet of gods and goddesses. Pure Orpheus was credited by his Hellenic descendants with the numinous drawing-down of the immortal godhead to the soul of man. By the wisdom and lineage of the "god-infilled Initiator," the immortal soul became the essential mark of being human. In that sense, he is the spiritual father of Sokrates, who then gave the soul modern individuality.

Orpheus was the first in the West to advocate a full-time devotion to the divine—not merely the social religion of cultural adherence, but a lifetime occupation of discrimination, devotion, and realisation. For the first time in the West, renunciation was possible as a religious path.

> *The wise man should merge his speech in his mind, and his mind in his intellect. He should merge his intellect in the Cosmic Mind, and the Cosmic Mind in the Tranquil Self.*
> — Katha Upanishad I. iii. 3

The golden sheets (the *lamella*) give us the triumphant voice of an Orphic adept in tones suggestively Upanishadic:

> *I have escaped from the sorrowful, weary round;*
> *I have entered the ring desired with eager feet;*
> *I have passed to the bosom of the goddess of the Underworld.*
> *Happy and Blessed*
> *My soul is immortal.*

In the seventh and sixth centuries BCE, the followers of Orpheus toured Hellas, teaching those who would enter into the disciplines of Orpheus. For the first time in the West, devotion to the divine life became a full-time possibility. The priests of Orpheus had no one holy ground or set temple, but they toured the land with scripture and with the demonstration of communion, meeting people in their own villas or huts, and they admonished their listeners to live an acetic life devoted to the divine. They carried the promise that those who fulfilled the personal and moral disciplines would enjoy the same ambrosial Remembrance of immortal ecstasy.

The *Orpheteletai*, or Initiating Priests of Orpheus, galvanized those who responded to their ecstasy and knowledge. Exposure to the ecstasy and realisation of the priest brought *telete*, or "initiation." Pausanias describes this initiator power thus: "Now in my opinion Orpheus was one who surpassed those who went before him in the composition of verses, and readed a position of great power owing to the conviction that he had discovered how to initiate one into communion with the gods, how to purify them from sin, to cure diseases and to avert divine vengeance."

This ecstasy was ritually augmented by the intoxicants of Dionysus. Their word to describe their spiritual practice was *bacchos*, meaning "rave". Guided by the initiated (*Orphetelete*), priests transmitted (*telete*) their Master's communion and ecstasy through literature, mysteries, lyrics, and celebratory music.

Interestingly, *telete* is rooted in *telos*, meaning completion, fulfillment. Yet *telete* is translated into Latin as *initiare*! To be initiated is to feel the completion! Thus the Way *begins* with the divine intimacy that is its goal.

To receive initiation (*telete*) was to feel the transmission of divine communion from the god-possessed Initiator. It was to see, feel, and remember the "constant ecstasy" of the Master. The *Orphetelete* radiated their ecstasy through sacred rites—bodily, emotionally, and intellectually communicating the joyous ground for remembrance (*anamnemisis*).

Marcus, in Cicero, *On the Laws*, 2.14.36, with reference to the transfomative power of the mysteries (of Eleusis):

> *For it appears to me that among the many exceptional and divine things your Athens has produced and contributed to human life, nothing is better that those mysteries. For by means of them we have been transformed from a rough and savage way of life to the state of humanity, and have been civilized. Just as they are called initiations, so in actual fact we have learned from them the fundamentals of life, and have grasped the basis not only for living with joy but also dying with a better hope.*

Orpheus reminded his listeners in flowing sutras, "song stitches," or *Rhap-sodies;* these *theological* rhapsodies served to purify the devotee of the Underworld's persuasions of fleshy logic and lazy indulgences so that joyous *anamnemisis*, the spiritual practice of remembrance became one's responsibility. When this remembering, regathering, religious practice became stable in sustained embrace, receiving fully and naturally loving, the *psyche* was illuminated by the *kosmic harmonia* and *theos* came to the soul. This *entheos* or "god infusion" enthusiastically established a rich ground for sweet remembrance.

What was remembered? The Bright Source at the Core of Everything, *Zeus* (Indo-European root: *dhyas*, "Bright"): the singular, self-existing, giving light of *Phanes*, the Clear Light of Reality, Bright-Zeus. "Out of the One the many, and out of the many, the One," goes the Orphic recitation.

The Bright divinity, Zeus, was not only a pre-rational, sentimental or mythic embrace for the sophisticated Hellene mystic, but also was a rational and trans-rational (theologos) intuition realized to be at the core of everything, the source of all, the blossoming radiance and singularity of *harmonia*. In the words of Herakleitos, "The Wise is One Only. It is willing and unwilling to be called by the name *'Zeus.'*"

Or, again, in the words of the ancient Orphics chanting Apollo's hymn,

*ZEUS EVERYWHERE—ZEUS EVERYWHERE—
ZEUS EVERYWHERE*

*Zeus the first, Zeus of the flashing lightning bolt
the last; Zeus the head, Zeus the middle, from
Zeus have all things been made. Zeus is the
foundation of the earth and of the starry heaven;
Zeus was male, Zeus was the immortal bride;
Zeus the breath of all things, Zeus the rush of the
flame unwearied; Zeus the source of the sea, Zeus
the sun and moon; Zeus the king, Zeus of the
flashing lightning, the beginning of all things. For
he concealed all and again brought them forth
from his sacred heart to the glad light, working
wondrous things.*

*ZEUS EVERYWHERE—ZEUS EVERYWHERE—
ZEUS EVERYWHERE*

Prior to Orpheus, *athanatos (immortality)*, was
the epithet of gods and goddesses and a few heroes,
like Heracles. Pure Orpheus brought it from the
godhead to the soul of man. This epochal change was
noted with ancient clarity by the famed classics
professor William Greene in his 1948 work *Moira*,
"The conception of the soul as divine, and the idea that
it comes into its rights only in sleep or after death, are
Orphic, and meet us here for the first time." By the
wisdom and lineage of the "god-infilled Initiator," the
immortal soul descended from the gods to the essence
of being human.

Harmonia **and** *Dike*

Faced with an immortal condition, the soul embraced a new commitment to morality. Upon the strength of a life balanced by the "ascetic" practices of temperance, followers of Orpheus grew in sensitivity to the vibrance of divine joy—the native joy that is distinct from body-based pleasures. They were transformed by this understanding into a new maturation and resonance — *harmonia*, defined in Orphism as "being in tune". This wisdom was called *sophia*; this temperance, *sophrosyne*. When the personal practice of *harmonia* grew sufficiently strong, then one resonated to the *harmonia* of the *kosmos*.

The *theologoi* spoke for the logic of divine existence (*theos logos*, theology), instead of the logic of body and belief. This theological preference for the soul's importance over the fleshy orientation was expressed repeatedly as *soma-sema*, usually translated as "the body is a tomb." It was through this chant (*soma-sema-soma-sema*) that Orpheus harped upon the immortality of the soul. Emphasizing the beyond-mere-body fountain of divinity, Orpheus emphasized attention to the soul's needs by disciplining the body.

But the root meaning of *sema* is "a sign," or "marks the spot," and by this significance became associated with "tomb." While the common understanding of *soma-sema* is "the body is a tomb," a further implication of "*soma-sema*" indicated a sensitivity to how one was presently buried in his or her own mechanical existence, or spindle destiny. Understanding this *already-underground,* ordinary suffering was indeed the first noble truth of both East *and* West. Plato/Socrates again summarizes, "Now some say that the body (*soma*) is the *sema* of the soul, as if it were buried in its present existence; and also because through it the soul makes signs it is rightly named *sema*." Be trapped and embedded in your present existence or let the soul show its signs of light and love with the body and mind.

Beyond the senses are the objects; beyond the objects is the mind; beyond the mind, the intellect; beyond the intellect, the Great Atman; beyond the Great Atman, the Unmanifest; beyond the Unmanifest, the Purusha, the Divine Person. Beyond the Purusha there is nothing: the Divine Person is the end, the Supreme Goal.
— Katha Upanishad I.iii.10–11

The feeling, breathing *psyche* of Hellas was called *atman* in Vedic India, and both are translated into English as *soul*. It was this emphasis of soul over mere body <u>and</u> mere sentiment that formed the soulful way to immortal happiness—both in the Upanishadic East and the Orphic West. (And both the Upanishads and Orphisim easily degrade into body-negativity and schismatic idealisms.)

Understanding the grave implications of fleshy logic would inspire the newly initiated, the *myste,* to renounce all but the soul's needs, pleasures, and sacrifices. A life wherein this recognition of bodily-oriented suffering and renunciation of illusion was absent was compared to "living in a dark cave" in Orphism. The classic metaphor of the cave is built upon this Orphic light.

"According to him," if a person would be attentive to their own blockage of the divine nature, and freely look upon the *stain* of their soul, then they could *abstain* from *adikia*—unjust acts. *Dike*, the righteous goddess of balance and justice, stood at the Gates of Hades and was "the Primal Way of Things," the required divine Way to the *kosmic harmonia*.

Prominent in Orphism is this goddess *Dike* (Justice), who "shared the same house as Hades"; they are both rooted in death. It was well noted that the divinity of balanced living was the first encounter in the mystic way through the darkness. Also resonating with the goddess *Dike* were the underworld "Judges of the Dead," who weighed the soul's oaths (*juris*) and deeds soon after the last breath.

The divinity of justice was also the means whereby the disbursement of power from the throne and the wealthy to the citizens was accomplished. Wise laws purified the society and made the city balanced. Orphics were famous for their law-giving.   Right and wrong, the simplest of indications, were known by *dikaios* and *ekdikos*. *Dike*, justice, balance, rightness— this divinity brought one next to the divine that is eternal joy.

"They who are righteous beneath the rays of the sun, when they die have a gentler lot in a fair meadow ..."

To cleanse the impurities, the *adikia,* from the soul, the recommended *purifications (katharsis)* were abstention, restraint, retribution (*nemesis*), and recompense. *Katharsis* was a cleansing that included moral acts, right diet, right relations, and right emotions. Fear and pity and anger were to be expressly purged along with the rest of injustice. As the pollution (*adikia*) was countered with right acts, a clearer body and mind would slowly appear, like rinsing a dirty sponge.

A practicing Orphic would make a commitment to forever confront and restrain the *adikia,* the unbalanced, unjust, addicted modes of dark sympathies—"the unreasonable, disorderly, and violent part of us". *Katharsis* was a spiritual work, a natural obligation of perpetual cleansing—a labor of refreshment that led to a spiritual clarity.

Many Orphic precepts revolved around the injunction to *katharsis,* or purification. This *katharsis* was explicitly described as the disciplined giving of one's soul to Dike, divine justice. By passing through this divine balancing and justice, and setting their feeling free, disciples began to awaken to immortal joy.

Freely feeling, the practitioners received the free awareness that was self-evidently the only light left after the last breath. "According to him," if balance and just ways were practiced while alive, the balancing divinity provided the way for feeling to become free (to the *aither*). From the Rhapsodies: "And all the others marvelled when they saw the unlooked-for light in the *aither*, so richly gleamed the body of immortal *Phanes* ['primal light']."

Aither, "the dazzling light of the sky," the etheric, was known in the East as *prana. Prana*, like *aither*, was associated with the breath and the breath-spirit of all living beings. Embracing the divinity of restraint and using the breath to weave the body, feeling, the mind, and primal joy, led the dedicated disciple to the liberation of feeling and an enhanced sensitivity to the all-pervading life.

Instead of unbalanced indulgence and exploitation, the Orphic practiced honor of all living beings, balanced restraint, and harmonious morality—and exclaimed ceremoniously, "Evil have I fled, better I have found."

The fulfillment of desires, the foundation of the universe, the endless rewards of sacrifices, the shore where there is no fear, that which is adorable and great, the wide abode, and the goal—all this you have seen; and being wise, you have with firm resolve discarded everything else.
    —Katha Upanishad I.ii.11

The expressed Orphic promise of this cleansing work was that all things would be released and shed that were not divine. Divine balance was the just foundation of being "god-infilled" (*entheos*), and coming to "open eyes" (*epopte*).

The golden sheets sing the Orphic liberation,

> *Out of the Pure I come*
> *I have paid the penalty for unrighteous deeds*
> *I have flown out of the sorrowful, weary Wheel of*
> *Generation*
> *I have passed with eager feet to the Circle desired*
> *Thou art become god from human.*

Through this purification and practice of communion, the nature of the world and oneself became transparent in a single joyous harmony, and divine-self realization was possible. In the words of the "poet-scientist" Empedokles, the Orphic torch-bearer and primary disciple of Pythagoras, "From what divine honor, what height of bliss come I, to wander in the land of mortals... I tell you I am a god immortal, no longer a mortal."

Over a century before the *birth* of Socrates, the "Purifying Priests of Orpheus" became widely influential as they went about the land with their many scrolls and ceremonies, dressed in white raiment, teaching the way, founding communal societies, and *purifying and healing* the land via their invocation of Dike — suggesting fair laws. (Later charlatans would give such service a bad name and received acrid disdain from Herakleitos, Plato/Socrates, and the playwrights.)

In the early sixth century (BCE), these priests were giving purifying laws (*Dike*) to "polluted" (*adikia*) cities. The most famous of these law-giving purifications was demonstrated by the Sage Epimenides, the "greatest spiritual master of all the magically-gifted men." At the behest of the Oracle at Delphi itself, Epimenides, "one of the ecstatic mystics," came to an Athens in 593 BCE, counseled the poet and statesman Solon in new, balanced laws; he performed rituals, taught openly, and "purified the city."

The three year plague ended, and Epimenides (noted, like Orpheus, for his "prolonged ecstasy") was hailed as the Liberator, *Eleutherios*. Historians give all the credit of Athen's leveling and invigoration to the political savvy of Solon, but anciently Epimenides was equally praised for this miracle. It can be presumed that his famous works on politics and ritual were composed then, and added to his widely acclaimed Theogony. (Neither of which have survived.) This spiritual and political balancing between the rich, the poor, and the growing middle class began the inevitable march to full democracy.

The Orphic Acme

The later half of the sixth century was a revival of the spirituality which had begun the century, and this revival was noted at Delphi, Eleusis, Athens, and in all the Dionysian and Orphic cults. Also during this

Orphic resurgence, just prior to the golden age, Peisistratus' (fl. 561-527) theosophical advisor, the genius Onomakritos, collected and recast the *Rhapsodes*, fully establishing Orphic canon. It is no wonder that Aristotle thought Onomakritos *was* Orpheus.

Onomakritos' legacy can also be seen in the marbling of the hillside seats below the Acropolis for the Orphic story of Dionysus (beginning theater in the West); and we can presume that it was the wisdom of Onomakritos that prompted Peisistratus to open the Eleusian Mysteries from the privileged royalty to everyone.

Onomakritos promoted Orphism as a high priest and, having the ear of the throne, had the power to disseminate the refreshed teachings of Orpheus to the colonies. Known as the "minister of cults," he served to establish Orphism in every Hellenic center. He was a great force in the dissemination of the many Orphic scrolls from Athens to the rest of the Hellenic world. From hometown Athens to Eleuthernai on Crete, to sacred Delphi, to Miletus, Thrace, and to the ashram of Pythagoras at Crotona, brief communities founded on Orphic principles flourished. Pythagoras' school is the archetypal, and most developed, Orphic renunciate society we know.

The influence of Orphism can be found in all the pre-Socratics and tragedians, but let it be pointedly repeated that upon the Orphic conception of the immortality of the soul, Plato cast his immortal Forms. Even Sokrates' cave was an Orphic cave. Plato was famous for his ability to quote the *Orphika* text, and his brilliant thought bequeathed the theological and religious thought of Orphism to all Western souls. With all of this in mind, let us not forget the *Upanishadic* influences upon the spirituality in the West, influences that transformed ancient Hellas from shamanic ravings into a mystical purity.

Literacy and Theology

"Lord Orpheus" and his disciples founded a new religion in his reformation of Dionysian worship, and it was said that his was the New Testament to the Olympian Cosmogony. The bardic, spoken word of myth was suddenly superseded by the literacy of Orpheus, breaking the spell of childish belief in the mystic dawn of a new realism.

A religion founded on books, not places, was a relatively new and suddenly widespread manifestation—with Indian, Hellenic, Levatine, and Asian developments. Prior to literacy, the sacred, oral teachings were usually studied only by those who had expressed a great desire and intent to live for (and with and in) the divine, and had been adopted by a truly great teacher. "*Upanishad*" means the teachings found "at the feet of" the enlightened One.

Through literacy, the intimate wisdom of the oral tradition became more widely available and scripture flourished. Empowered by literacy, the wall around the palace became the wall around the city and the palaces became sacred Temples. The knowledge reserved for royalty and the wealthy was now open in the Holy Center. The rule of the king was replaced by the rule of law. At the leading edge of culture, adult authencity and mystic revelation replaced the mythic modalities of common membership. Literacy was a revolution.

The written teachings of Lord Orpheus were effective on a personal level as it broadened the disciple into a deeper being with a higher enjoyment. Socially, it transformed the parental power of the bardic story into a self-empowering literacy, and, in doing so, introduced spiritual authority to the reader.

Orphism was noted for its body of literature, the *Orphika.* To be an Orphic was a life-long commitment to study a "mass of books," and to feel, reason, and realize the truth therein communicated. To be an Orphic was the epitome of learning. Euripides noted of the Orphic followers, "They do not eat meat, they honor the rites of Dionysus, they honor many books, and they have Orpheus for their Master."

It was said that Orpheus was the first and brightest of the theological poets (*theologoi*), whose precepts and principles stepped beyond the mythic mind of belief to a theological *nous*—an ecstatic, mystic understanding (*gnosis).*

Prior to the *theologoi*, only poets and bards (like Homer) mythically sang of the divine, but the *theologoi* communicated the divine wisdom in both sacred story and logical clarity. Theological authority revised the sacred story with a fresh voice—a voice made true by a lineage of divine realizers (creating scripture in their wake). Theology was the "literal" bridge between mythology and philosophy. Walter Burkett, in his seminal work, *Greek Religion*, emphasized the transfomative force of this theology, "Orphic literacy takes hold in a field that had previously been dominated by the immediacy of ritual and the spoken word of myth. The new form of transmission introduces a new form of authority to the individual....The emancipation of the individual and the appearance of books go together ..."

Blessed Orpheus, the one who possessed "the secrets of Hades," amended the cosmogony, illuminated the nature of the Underworld, and literally gave the Hellenes a new world view: To the spatial cosmology of Hesiod, Orpheus added temporality: the knowledge of destinies and the wisdom of associating with divinity. With the immortality of the soul, the injunction for morality was absolute.

The one who spoke with the Lord of Death gave humankind access to the eternal domain, beyond waking, sleeping, dreaming, and dying. The one who witnessed "stillness in dark places" and the "soul of deep sleep" changed what was understood about the vibrant way of divine awakening.

Orpheus reportedly began his day with an austerity apparently learned from the Indian yogis: rising before the sun and walking to a spot where the sunrise could be seen. In predawn slowness, the yogis would go through a routine of postures to awaken and harmonize the body. Breathing practices would inspire the pranic, etheric energies and feelings to rush through inward and outward pathways. As the life-force vaulted awake and sunlight broke forth, the practitioners looked into the horizon sunshine, letting the soft star relax into their sight with their in-breath. Closing the eyes and breathing inward with skyward feelings, the yogis would exhale and swoon upwards to the creative bright star at the mystic origin of the body and all things. Orpheus was noted for this practice.

Orpheus, the "god-infilled Initiator," founded western spirituality by blending Upanishadic enlightenment with the Homeric/Hesiodic religiosity of the Hellenes. With an empowering Orphic step forward, *mythos* transformed to *hiero logos*, or sacred and moral story, then to mystic *ek-stasis*, ecstasy — *the* evidence of divine intercourse. Ecstasy gave birth to the immortal soul (*psyche*), speech about the blossoming being (*physis*), and divine reason (*theologos*). Theogonies flourished, all inspired by the prophet Orpheus. "The legends of Orpheus are sacred song, the other world, and the ennobling a man by song and transcendence, by the mysteries and the divine suffering of the founder."

The feeling, breathing *psyche* of Hellas was called *atman* in Vedic India, and both are translated into English as *soul*. It was this emphasis of soul over mere body <u>and</u> mere sentiment that formed the soulful way to immortal happiness—both in the Upanishadic East and the Orphic West.

Orpheus was well-known for his soulful tempering (*sophrosyne*) of the raving rites (*bacchos*). With the advent of *sophrosyne*, Orpheus incarnated the dynamic dance of still Apollo and energetic Dionysus in person. His power was the *dynamis* of the two gods in a single being, and he was likened to the Temple at Delphi itself (where the Hellenes housed Apollo and Dionysus together).

It has been said that Delphi itself was only fully baptised and empowered with the Orphic "Dionysation of Delphi." Indeed, upon the *lesche* wall of Polygnotos at the Delphi was Orpheus revealing the realm of Hades. And also there, upon a recovered metope is Orpheus with his lyre assisting the Argonauts, giving the adventurers more power than brute force could deliver, more power than even clever cunning could conceive, more enchantment than the call of sirens. With his heart-lyre, Orpheus even calmed the waters of the stormy sea, and called down sleep upon the eyes of the untamed dragon which guarded the Golden Fleece—all through his "god-infilled" joy.

Orpheus, the mad priest of love, was far more than the mythical and magical minstrel who could charm and move men, gods, trees, and even stones. Rather, his songs, legends, and myths belong to a body of spiritual instruction, and, together with abundant fragments of the *Orphika*, it seems obvious that Orpheus was a powerful spiritual teacher—a communicator of wise liberation with a wide impact.

As the "Reformer," Orpheus recast the cosmogony and cosmic order, such that the kosmos, instead of coming out of Darkness or Night, was first born of Primal Light, Self-Existing Brightness (*Phanes*), and Love—from which the Gods, Goddesses, and humanity would come.

Amending the spatial "Hesiodic" framework with the fateful sense of time-flow, Orpheus challenged his followers to comprehend the destiny of their choices. The new Orphic cosmogony challenged the moral and immortal soul. "According to him", even Chaotic Dark is illumined by the seed of spiritual Love. More important that all other cosmological revisions, Orpheus added Love, *Eros* (known also in its lighted sense as *Phanes)*. *Eros* joined Night, embracing even *Chaos* ("gap", "void") with divine communion. Thus, Eros, Night, and Chaos were known as "Orphic powers."

The orthodoxical Aristophanes captures for us the common Orphic cosmological description:

> *It was Chaos and Night at the first,*
> *and the blackness of darkness,*
> *and Hades' broad border.*

Earth was not, nor air, neither heaven,
when in the depths of the womb (delphi)
of the dark without order
First thing first-born
of the black--plumed night was a wind-egg
hatched in her bosom,
Whence timely with seasons revolving again
sweet Love burst out as a blossom

Gold wings gleaming forth of his back (Phanes),
like whirlwinds gustily turning,
He, after his wedlock with Chaos,
whose wings are of darkness,
in Hades broad-burning

For his nestlings begot him the race of us first,
and upraised us to light new-lighted.

And before this was not the race of the gods,
until all things by Love were united:
And of kind united with kind
in communion with nature, the sky and the sea.
The blessed are Brought forth
and the earth and the race of the gods are blest
and everlasting.

The *Orphika* was fully developed by the sixth century, and was known in several forms, such as "Hymns", "Songs", "Sacred Stories" (*Heiros Logos*) and "Rhapsodies." The *rhap-sodes,* or "song stitches" were philosophically and etymologically resonant to the "thread" of Hindi "sutras," and also the etymological root of today's medical "thread," "sutre." Orpheus' threads, *sodes,* were full of flow (*rhea*), weaving the fabric of truth, musing the revelation, dancing upon a point again and again in joyous demonstration. The rhapsodies were the first teachings to be known as the wisdom attentive to the very divine, *theo-logos.*

As a spiritual teacher, Orpheus described the Bright numinous divinity that can be found in both the death process and in the mystic passage through the dark unconsciousness, revealing Elysium, "the abode of divinity." As a rationalist, Orpheus elucidated the evolutionary structure of the kosmos. He suggested that life came out of "water and slime warmed by the sun," then evolved through higher animals until the purified human form. As a realist, he required the understanding of suffering rather than belief in myths in order to serve one's attunement to the unlimited. He rearranged the Western conception of the afterlife, taught *palingenesis* (reincarnation of the soul), and spawned a soulful emergence of individualism.

The rising individuality transmitted by this Upanishadic/Orphic gift of soulful immortality began a new turning of the world, and civilization was refreshed and moved forward. Mythological modes of orientation were exceeded by theosophical doctrines, where individual insight outshined membership belief.

Speculative theology and prophetic speech brought forth the theological birth of *logos*, reason. This divine knowledge is *gnosis*–linked etymologically to Vedanta's *jnana*, "divine knowledge," and also to Arabic *jnna*, "divine madness," from which we get "genius".

Orpheus' transformed and transforming influence went down the west coast of Asia Minor to Ionia and became physics and metaphysics; his cosmogony and mystic gnosis went south to Athens and became the Rhapsodies, philosophy, theatre, and democracy; his enlightened joy moved west to Italy and emerged in harmony, mathematics, community, Stillness, and Being without genesis. The influence of Orpheus and Orphism can hardly be overstated.

Orpheus could be called the first Dharma-Bearer to the West, and philosophy's first light. Indeed, the soul of Orpheus can be found in Anaximander's necessity and justice, in "Law-Giver" Parmenides' poem of Being, in Herakleitos' *Logos*, and in Socratic ignorance, epistemology, and soulfulness. Then Plato's metaphysics gave it a classical form which has lasted for thousands of years. To look out of your eyes, feeling that you are a soul, being mysteriously led to the Light, is to see the effect of Orpheus now.

Listen!

It has been suggested that the word *Orpheus* is rooted in ορϕνε, "chthonic dark." If this is true, then it can be said that *accepting* and *knowing the darkness* is coincident with light. This stillness in dark places and light-piercing-the-darkness (Hindi *gu-ru*) is the herald-call of human maturation. Blessed Company awaits all who heed the invitation.

Myste also implied that one should close the mouth and <u>listen</u> to the word of One who is Awake beyond the dreams of Hades. *Myste*! (Listen!) When asked why new initiates to his company had to keep silent and only *listen* to the Master for five years, Pythagoras answered, "Like cloth is whitened before dyes color it."

To receive initiation (*myste*) was to accept adoption by a god or master—it was to be re-born to another fate beyond your common destiny. To submit to the grace of a divine being and receive his or her blessings was what was meant to be a *myste*. *Myste* is rooted in *myeo*, "to close," and the social suggestion is to close your mouth and keep secret the mysteries, like intimate knowledge. *Myste* carries the implication of "secret," a heartful respect for initimate, mysterious "knowing". Listen to the Testament of Secrets and receive the Mysterious Initiation of a Master!

This sensitivity to the lineage of wisdom was the school of character, to answer the noble (*ariste*) call of excellence (*arete*). (And the Four Noble Truths of Gautama are the Four *Aryan* Truths. Those who answered this call harvested the "wisdom of suffering" (παθει μαθοσ). Otherwise, as Adi Da Samraj points out, "Suffering just leads to more suffering.")

Arise! Awake! Approach the great and learn.
Like the sharp edge of a razor is that path, so the wise
say, hard to tread and difficult to cross.
— Katha Upanishad I.iii.14

Embrace requires a partial closure, the exercise of restraint, of dear tempering (*sophrosyne)* and taming the outgoing energies of a dissipated life, likened to taming a steed. To be a *myste*, an initiate, was a great and honored challenge to divine living. Intimacy, listening, discrimination, and temperance characterized the life recommended by the Master of the mysteries.

If the buddhi, being related to a distracted mind, loses its discrimination and therefore always remains impure, then the embodied soul never attains the goal, but enters into the round of births.
But if the buddhi, being related to a mind that is restrained, possesses discrimination and always remains pure, then the embodied soul attains that goal from which he is not born again.
A man who has discrimination for his charioteer, and hold the reins of the mind firmly, reaches the supreme goal.
— Katha Upanishad I.iii.7–9

The *myste* understood the necessity to listen, not just to the Master, but to their stream of experience. To develop sensitivity to one's participation in the play of experience was the quintessence of the *myste's* "purifications." One who listens, hears. Listening to the unbalanced, out of tune actions, one is graced with sensing the resonant truth. Indeed, one order of renunuciates under Pythagoras was referred to as the *Akoustomaki*—"the Hearers."

The self-revelations encountered in the ascetic way Orpheus recommended empowered the *myste* to a realistic self-understanding. Similar to the awareness of *dukkis*, or the First Noble Truth of the Buddha, a sensitivity to the root of suffering. Practitioners East and West were called to listen in order to hear.

What is here, the same is there; and what is there, the same is here. He goes from death to death who sees any difference here.
—Katha Upanishad II.i.9

The Spindle Destiny

Orpheus, "the great realizer of Dionysus," came "full of god," and proclaimed the secret way beyond the usual destiny and death. His mythic description of the underworld contained a description of the passage beyond the prisons of life and afterlife, as well as liberation from the mechanics of destiny.

Well then, I shall tell you about this profound and eternal Brahman, and also about what happens to the atman after meeting with death.
— Katha Upanishad II.ii.6

According to Orpheus, lord of the mysteries, the soul comes into the body with the first breath, and when the body expires, the *psyche*, breath or spirit no longer animates the body. Life flows out of the body, dissolving flesh and thinking—as the "shade" emerges from the top of the head (or out of the mouth with the last breath). Hermes, the "Crosser of all Boundaries," comes with his magic staff to take the "shade" or soul (*psyche*) on its journey. There is the inherent cognition that the staff of Hermes is the mystical path up and out of the body, and likewise there is the recognition that the inexorable flow of death is the river Styx.

After the body and mind are left behind, the only quality that remains is one of thirst. It is the thirst or need that moved one while alive to be fulfilled. Now the yearning is without an object; neither wealth, nor adoration, nor sexuality, nor glory, nor pleasure of any kind obscures the naked unfulfilled need itself.

Thus possessed of a naked thirst, the tour of the previously un-seen (*a-des* "Hades") begins. First, *Dike* and the Judges of the Dead judge or weigh the oaths (*juris*) the souls made during life to see how well oaths were kept: this weighing was known as *psychestasis*. (This is essentially identical to the Egyptian description of balancing the soul's heart against a feather.)

Coming to depth of self-knowledge too late, most souls are tormented, confused, and driven about the Underworld. Pindar sings of this *psychestasis* after death,

The guilty souls of the dead straightway pay the penalty (for missing the mark of the heart) *here on earth, and the acts that miss the mark committed in this kingdom of Zeus are judged by the One beneath the ground.*

The "shade" wanders further down into the muddy darkness of Hades and soon comes upon the Pool of *Lethe* (Forgetfulness). Those souls whose habit of immediate satisfaction dominated their heart while alive desperately throw themselves upon the shores of Lethe to satisfy their driving thirst.

Drinking from the waters of *Lethe*, their need *is* satisfied, but they forget who they are and wander forever aimlessly and in confusion throughout the Underworld—in the muddy, flatland of Asphodel— where neither trees nor any of the fruits of the earth appear.

Satisfying new thirsts by drinking from the river of Indifference ("been there, done that"), un-lighted souls eventually gather in the meadow of *Tartarus*. There, they journey the Milky Way to the celestial axis of *Ananke* (Necessity), where her daughter, the Fate *Lachesis* (who presides over lots), gave each soul a "*daimon* appropriate to his choice."

To understand the interplay of the Fate *Lachesis* and the soul is critical. The soul must choose its *daimon*, its character, which *Lachesis* then assigns to the soul as his

or her "guardian and the fulfiller of his choice." Thus, the soul and Fate, self and luck, free will and embeddedness, future choices and the "tragic tense" share responsibility for the fabric of life. (And this leads to the later-in-life wisdom of knowing what you can and cannot change.)

The *daimon* leads the soul to another daughter of Zeus and Necessity, the Fate *Clotho* (the spinner)—who turns the spindle to ratify the destiny that the soul got "by choice and by lot". The soul then receives the "inflexible" news of his or her eventual atrophy and termination from the final divine daughter, Fate *Atropos* ("she who cannot be turned"), "who makes the web of destiny irreversible."

As the three daughters of Necessity, together with the *sirens* (lit. "to bind") sang the fate of the soul in the music of the spheres, souls were again brought before the throne of Necessity. The way to rebirth began and ended with Necessity. At the knees of Necessity rested the Spindle which governed the movement of incarnation into the *kosmos*—arising in concentric spheres or "whorls"—according to the fates and gravity of necessity.

The souls destined for reincarnation were made to drink again from the waters of Lethe, so that their recollection of their previous life and Underworld experience dimmed and was forgotten. Thus rendered lethargically unconscious, souls are thrust into a new incarnation, to try again and learn the wise way (*philosophia*) to divine reason (*nous*) and thereby immortality. To be liberated from the mere "cycle of generation" was the lesson and challenge by which the transmigrating soul (*metempsychosis*) would pass out of the dreamy afterlife into a dreamy birth and breathe again.

> *Some enter the womb for the purpose of new embodiment, and some enter into stationary objects—according to their work and according to their knowledge.*
> — Katha Upanishad II. ii.7

Upon the first breath, each soul is imprinted with its "spindle destiny," the implied fate of everything surrounding the newborn. One's "spindle destiny" was spun from the threads of mother, father, family, village, language, culture—even the sun, moon, and stars. (In India, this spindle destiny is known as *karma* within the net of *maya*).

To penetrate the spindle destiny was the great challenge in moving beyond "the tomb of ordinary destiny" to a free divinity. Such penetrating authenticity was the trademark of the *theologoi*. In the words of Plato, the *theologoi* were "divine men, who may be expected to know the truth about their own parents." (Here we can also recall Herakleitos' injunction, "Do not be the child of your mother and father.") Moving beyond our spindle destiny by disciplining our own inherited cloth and re-actions, we mature into present responsiveness, beyond ego/I and the tomb or ordinary destiny. True response-ability.

Plotinus made this quite discernment quite clear in answering a devotee's question about astrology. (11.3.9), "In every moment you have a choice: you can live your Spindle destiny or you can live authentically." To live authentically will mature into the simplicity that outshines the Spindle destiny; not eliminating it, but turning beyond ego-orientation into real relationship. To live authentically is to outshine mechanical reaction in responsive mutuality; intercoursing with presence rather than attacking/exploiting or pulling back in fear. To live authentically is a kind of always present deathlessness, even while the textures and threads of our Spindle destiny pass away.

From the Icy Halls of Hades to the Riches of Pluto

With the advent of Orpheus, death ceased to be a grey copy of life on earth like it was portrayed in Homer (and the Near East mythologies). With mystic Orphism, death became another moment in an eternal process whereby one can look up from the pool of changes and suddenly be already awake.

On the Orphic sheets of pure gold, or *lamellae,* we find awake awareness about the transcendence (or utter acceptance) of feared Hades and death, and how to be awake in the afterlife, and what that means for living now. We read the injunctions to a divine life here, injunctions on how we should live to best serve the immortal soul. The rhapsodies of Orpheus not only taught purification and balance, they empowered the soul to choose paradise while living —as well as when the body falls away. From the *lamellae,*

> *And the Kings under the earth will pity you,*
> *and they will give you to drink from the lake of Remembrance.*
> *And it is a thronged road you are setting out on,*
> *a holy one along which other famous initiates and bacchants are proceeding.*
> *Thou shalt find to the left in the House of Hades the Pool of Forgetfulness*
> *To this well-spring do not approach,*
> *Look up to the white poplar*
> *There find another water-source, the Lake of Remembrance.*
> *Cool water flows there, surrounded by Guardians.*
> *Finding the Pool of Remembrance, approach and say:*
> *"I am the offspring of Earth and starry Sky,*
> *"I am parched with thirst and am dying;*
> *"Quickly give me the cool waters flowing forth from Remembrance."*

Those that drink of the waters there go to the same immortal place as the Heroes and also take on the mantel of divinity.
(more in Appendix: The Lamella)

This passage to Elysium was discovered and cultivated in the ancient mystery schools, giving the initiated *myste* great joy while alive and imparting a mysterious understanding of the process of death. For those initiated into the sacred feeling of Belovedness (the basis for Rembrance), the privilege of Elysium was transferred from the province of the afterlife's Underworld to glorious living on the surface of the Earth.

Orphic knowledge became widespread under the zeal of Onomakritos — when he opened the mysteries at Eleusis with its psychotropic *kykeon* to every free Hellene. Suddenly, everyone had the ceremonies, and access to the experiential basis of the propagandized cosmogonies.

This point is clearly illucidated for us by Stobaios:

The soul [at the point of death] has the same experience as those who are being initiated into the great mysteries . . . At first one wanders and wearily hurries to and fro, and journeys with suspicion through the dark as one uninitiated: then come all the terrors before the final initiation, shuddering, trembling, sweating, amazement; then one is struck with a marvelous light, one is received into pure regions and meadows, with voices and dances and the majesty of holy sounds and shapes; among these he who has fulfilled initiation wanders free, and released and bearing his crown joins in the divine communion, and consorts with pure and holy people.

It is worthy of note that the word *Hades* is from *Aides* (*a-des*), meaning not-day, not bright, dark unconscious, fearful un-known. Its qualities are of shadowy, lazy forgetting, dark and fearful not-knowing; fearful not-accepting; lamentful, un-fulfilled thirsting; shortsighted foolishness; and lethal arrogance. The domain of Hades holds the grave unknown and the unconscious dark.

Interestingly, the Lord of the Underworld was also referred to as the "Most Gracious One," since He received every soul with open arms. An Orphic hymn invokes Him:

Pluto! Subterranean is your dwelling place, O strong-spirited one...
All-Receiver, with death at your command, you are master of mortals...
You delight in the worshipper's respect and reverence. Come with favor and joy to the initiates, I summon you.

When the darkness was illuminated by purification and faith, and the unconscious was no longer resisted or covered, when fear, pity, and anger allowed themselves to be known, seen, and accepted, then feared Hades became luminous Pluto, the god of riches. Thus it is said, "Where one stumbles, there one finds the treasure."

Pluto is the name for Hades when his darkness is lighted, revealing the jewels and gold beneath the earth. The Hades-to-Pluto transition is the first hope of every soul.

The power and transformation of Hades held a mighty power in the minds of the ancient wise. From Zeus-Chthonios to Dionysus-Chthonios, from the Kathartic Asklepios to heroic Herakles, from sweet Persephone to the *mysteria* of Apollo, Dionysus, Eleusis, and Orpheus, Hades was a divinity with which to be reconciled and combined in order to be fully alive and to freely die.

In the words of Pindar,

Blessed is he who hath seen these things before he shall pass beneath the ground. He knoweth the end of life, and he knoweth this god-given origin.

This transformation from dark trouble to gracious riches was emphasized by Orpheus as he repeated the famous saying to convey the overwhelming fullness of real existence: "like a [thirsty goat] kid who has fallen into milk." The presumed tragedy and fear was suddenly found to be a blessing and overwhelming joy. Incarnation is not a grave matter only—it is an unfathomable blessing, the ecstatic place of divine intercourse.

Orpheus and Eurydice

Orpheus' well-known passage through Hades' Underworld for his Eurydice transmits the spiritual lessons on the power *and* the limits of human love. A spectrum of self-knowledge graces those who thoroughly examine the kinds and stages of love.

Orpheus' joy was clearly no ordinary affection. Indeed, this heart-joy was to be distinctly seen as being beyond common sentiment. His was the truly powerful love that mastered the urgent animals, the cyclical elements, the sentimental sirens, and even the problem of death. But still that powerful love had a limitation, the requirement of the other. So long as the Beloved is other, the dyadic lovers will be shattered by death. It is this dyadic tension of self and other, I and Thou, that possessed the mythical Orpheus to turn too quickly.

Orpheus, Eurydice, and Hermes

The lesson of Eurydice is the lesson on balancing the three loves: sentiment, real love, and spiritual love. This three-folded spectrum of heart-knowledge was the context wherein the Orphic located his true self-knowledge (confluent with the three-fold way of purification, communion, and ecstasy). To grow beyond the limits of object-dependency, human love, and religious deification comes from this Orphic insight into the dyadic error. This purification of sentiment into real love and the maturation of real love into divine love was the deeper lesson learned from Orpheus, Eurydice, and Hades.

Orpheus' mature demonstration of real love beyond brawn and sirens revealed the strength of real love in contrast to the ordinary weakness of immature sentiment. Orpheus' eventual loss of Eurydice revealed the limitation of human love: as long as the Beloved is Other, the love will be shattered. By the lesson of Orpheus and Eurydice, we are called to grow beyond sentiment and even human maturation into divine love. Sentiment is transformed by *katharsis* into real love, and human maturity is further purified by the "invasion of divinity" (*entheos*) to the soulful love of the divine.

The three loves were the three stages of the soul: sentiment, psyche, and divine self-realization. The deepest soul which witnesses the three common states—waking, dreaming, and sleeping—comes into its own in death, but can be sensed in deep sleep, and learned in mystical self-realization.

Later Christian theologians would echo this maturation of love via the ancient Hellenic words *eros* and *agape*. *Eros*, in the narrow Christian view, was the limited love of sentimental promises, sexual indulgence, and hopeful fulfillment; *agape* was the free love of self-giving, soulful sacrificial, sacred love. (*"Eros"* to the ancient Orphic ranged from the erotic multiplicity to the mystic's heart thrill of kosmic unity.)

When all the desires that dwell in the heart fall away, then the mortal becomes immortal and here attains Brahman.

When all the ties of the heart are severed here on earth, then the mortal becomes immortal. This much alone is the teaching.

The inner Self, always dwells in the hearts of men. Let a man separate Him from his body with steadiness, as one separates the tender stalk from a blade of grass. Let him know that Self as the Bright, as the Immortal—yes, as the Bright, as the Immortal.

Having received this wisdom taught by the King of Death, and the entire process of yoga, Nachiketa became free from impurities and death, and attained Brahman. Thus it will be also with any other who knows, in this manner, the inmost Self.

—Katha Upanishad II.iii. 14–15, 17–18

The Mystic Tour

Orpheus revealed another wonderful possibility beyond the tomb of being given to one's spindle destiny: the souls who enjoyed "the pleasure in the keeping of oaths," and who were made sufficiently light by the divinely oriented life were not lost in vast chasms after death, not mired in the muddy flats of Tartaros, but were given avenue to the Paradise of Elysium, "eternal drunkenness," the Islands and Company of the Blessed.

Learning the passage through the echoing halls of icy Hades was of utmost importance to the Orphics — for then the soul was liberated from fear, death, and all the spindled labors on the wheel of birth.

Souls who were initiated into divine knowledge while alive knew not to settle for the first satisfaction that came along. Instead, they looked away from the waters of Lethe and turned their eyes upward and looked to the white poplar tree. For those seriously prepared, the bright rapture of this transmission mysteriously illuminated the nervous system of the devotee as a white tree of life — seen internally in mystical vision as the dual-snaked herald of Hermes, the "Crosser of All Boundaries." Because this mystical vision of the white tree and nectarous soma graced those who utterly submitted to the divine while alive, it was purported to be seen in the process of death as the way whereby one finds the liberating Pool of Remembrance.

This is the eternal Asvattha Tree with its root above and branches below. That root ball, indeed is called the Bright; That is Brahman, and That alone is the Immortal. In that all worlds are contained, and none can pass beyond. This verily is That.
— Katha Upanishad II.iii.1

The soul arrives at the white tree and comes upon the Pool of Mnemnosyne, the waters of Heart Remembrance in the center of the brain. Here (at the Bright root ball of the Asvattha Tree), desire is finally vanquished by the sweetest of nectars, quenching and anointing every human and evolutionary thirst with baptismal sublimity.

Rising in radiant fullness from this divine pool, the wings of the Caduceus unfold within the mystical brain, crowning one's own heart-flight into the blissful paradise.

Let us listen again to the songs of Pindar, singing across the millennia the vision of Elysium that Initiates enjoy,

For them in the world below the sun shineth in his strength...and in meadows red with roses the space before their city is shaded with trees of frankincense, and is laden with fruits of gold. Some of them take delight in horses and in sports, and some with games of draughts and with lyres, and among them bloometh in perfection with the flower of bliss.

Over the lovely land fragrance is ever shed, as they mingle all manner of incense with the far-shining fire on the altars of the gods...
Flowers gleam bright with gold, with glorious trees, and wreaths intertwine their arms and crown the head.

This "crowning" was known in the Orphic schools as *stephanos*, and when one's cup overflowed in divine ecstasy, this was ceremoniously celebrated with garlands of laurel. Orphics were noted for their laurel crowns, indicating someone who had drunk from the divine Pool of Heart Remembrance, and had thus awakened into the consciousness of the divine domain. (In later times, the laurel indicated someone who was merely drinking freely or simply drunk.)

As clarified by Adi Da Samraj Eleutherios in *The Enlightenment of the Whole Body*, the top ball of the Caduceus is the mnemonic pool of nectarous soma at the pineal center of the brain (in India, the *ajna* door, amd the root ball of the Asvattha Tree), and the staff and snakes are the spine and nervous system harmonies. (Anatomically, the spine is represented by the straight staff, and sympathetic and parasympathetic portions of the nervous system are represented by the interwoven snakes. In India, yogis call these the *sushuma, ida* and *pingala*). The Caduceus is an image of the nervous

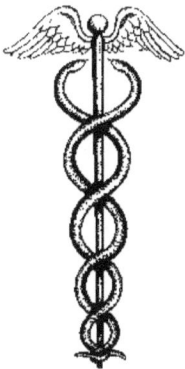

system in its native and divinely open state, the balanced soul perfectly alive.

In mystical ascent within the heart's thrill, one follows the white tree upwards and finds the rapturous pool. We drink the nectar of supreme being until every thirst is undone. According to the mystic teachings, as we rise from the nectarous Pool of Mnemnosyne, the vision of Bright Elysium's spirit-filled paradise exalts the soul, allowing heart nectar to light the ventricles of the brain — where their lightedness appears as the wings within. This mystical vision, felt and seen in the sublimnities of rising and rapturous love, has given cause for religious traditions (from Orphic mysticism and the traditional yogas of India to the Chinese Secret of the Golden Flower) to value the crowning terminus of the nervous system as the very divine.

> *He, the Supreme Divine Person in the Heart, who remains awake while the sense-organs are asleep, shaping one lovely form after another, is indeed the Pure; He is Brahman, and He is Immortal. All worlds are contained in Him, and none can pass beyond. This, verily, is That.*
> —Katha Upanishad II. ii. 8

For the mystic Orphics, the divine pool of Mnemnosyne or Remembrance at the entrance to Elysium was found in both mystical ascent and in the process of death. They loudly noted that to drink the waters of Remembrance, one must forsake the lethargic waters of Lethe. For the Orphics, to forsake the lethargic satisfactions of bodily pleasures and remember the ambrosial satisfaction of the soul's deepest thirst is the gateway to Paradise, or "eternal god-intoxication" (Vedanta, *samadhi*), whereby death is "swallowed up in victory," and the Orphic soul falls into "the unbroken radiance of divinity".

The Truth of Alethia

The understanding of the spiritual process whereby one turns up from Lethe (Forgetfulness or Coveredness) can be appreciated in the ancient Hellenic word for "truth, " *alethia.* In this most salient of all philosophic words, we find a deep understanding of the process of initiation/responsibility revealed in the Orphic schools. *Alethia, a-lethia, a-lethe*, not *Lethe*, not forgetful, not covered, not lethargic, not lethal—*alethia*, revelatory Truth, our Vibrant Reality as it Is.

Understanding the lethargic underworld and understanding the immortal worlds is just a metaphor for understanding the real truth of existence now. This in not merely everything altogether or anything un-masked, the real truth is what is always and already the case, beyond interior and exterior. When every subjective projection is un-covered, the presumptive error between within and all the world dissolves. As Adi Da says, "The Truth is not interior to the body. It is the Condition of the whole body-being. Thus, that

Condition is the native view toward or relative to the whole body-being and all conditions."

Orpheus' theological understanding of reality can be found in the insight of the lovers of wisdom, the *philosophers.* For the ancient lovers of wisdom, Lethe was coveredness and forgetfulness, while its opposite, *alethia,* was the revealing truth. Truth becomes visible when all the coverings are removed. To realize the Truth was undo all of our coverings and then look up from the ephemeral pool of driven-self-obsession.

Truth, in Orphic regard, is in no way limited to the factual or material; the implication of *alethia* was closer to spiritual work, conscious understanding, divine revelation, noble being; rememberance, and paradise. Alethia's uncovered, un-forgetful, un-lazy quality bespeaks of the wise ones who look up from themselves, who look up from the lethargic pool of lethal self-satisfaction. Truth is to un-cover, look up, and remember the perfect relatedness and singularity of divine existence.

The Death and Limitations of Orpheus

By the fifth century, the religion of Orphism as a whole had lost much of its purity and discrimination, and was scorned for its disdainful fakery and indulgent illusions. By the late fourth century, differences between the representations of Orpheus and Apollo disappeared, and the legend of Orpheus faded into the mythological background. Mythic Apollo harmonized with the inspired poet, until they became one.

Mythologically, it was reported that the wild women ravers of Dionysus became mad at Orpheus' allegiance to Apollo and tore Orpheus apart — in the manner that the god Dionysus had been ripped asunder. Apollo's Muses gathered his body, and his head was said to have survived intact, still spouting oracles (*nekymanteion*, lit. "manna of death"). And with this telling, it was repeated again that the process of the mysteries and the process of death are the same. Giving up everything is the entrance fee.

While an inner circle of serious disciples nurtured and passed on the spiritual force for centuries, Orphism became mostly known for its relentless search for purity, for its body-distrusting disharmony, for its schismatic and schizophrenic approach to life. Instead of the blissful unity of god-infilling, Orphics were obsessed with solving the problem of existence!

A thousand years after Orpheus tamed the mysteries, in the post-Plotinus darkness, and after the Imperial forces of the Roman Christians snuffed out the sacred rites, magicians incanted the name of Orpheus to empower a potion, and the Fields of Elysium was a heaven found only after death, or in some new, future age. Orphism was certainly dead.

Western Orphic Presumptions

Our gifts from the Orphic tree are many. It is the Orphic Dionysus who transformed from being *Zagreus,* "torn-apart," into a pleasure-loving goat, and then into a god—and, by this story, Western theatre was created. Orphism gave us theology and the theological bridge from mythology to philosophy. The Western presumption that there is an afterlife of consciousness and retribution where the soul makes conscious decisions is Orphic. Likewise, our presumption while alive that we are a "soul", a psyche within, is profoundly "Orphic" for Westerners. That we are an immortal soul inside and engage the flow of time as a morality play of wisdom and destiny could be described as "Orphic". The idea that the force of love exceeds the binding power of sirens is "Orphic". To feel the power and the limitation of human love is an "Orphic" issue. To court the Muses is Orphic, as it is to dare the underworld for love. To view the ordinary round of life as cavelike is Orphic, as is to think of the light outside the cave as divine. To conceive of heaven or eternal wholeness as wise and pleasurable is "Orphic". To follow the caduceus within as a mystic ascent of rapture is "Orphic". To understand and discern the Truth is central to our souls.

On the negative side, to have a negative relationship to the body is "Orphic". In that same vein, Orphism was pointedly misogynistic — until the reformation of Pythagoras. To turn away from life is

Orphic. To turn away from the world as a requirement of spirituality is Orphic. Orphism suffers all the limitations of religious and mystical paths to God: a dualistic conceptualization that this world and the body are bad, and the solution to human suffering is renunciation of this world and the body and to give your attention to the soul only. In accordance with this negative view of this world, it is from Orphism, via Christianity, we have inherited the tormenting afterlife in hell.

While there is much wisdom in this view, the truth is not schismatic. Even the Orphic realization was "to find oneself already in the Fields of Elysium," and Orpheus himself is said to describe realization as beginning "the years of pleasure." But while the realization speaks for the non-dual, unitive joy, the Orphic teaching is dualistic and schismatic, revealing its immaturity in the history of religious thought.

This negative view has contaminated Western thought, and was joined by similar contaminations of the Christians, and is only recently begun to abate. To revisit Orphism is to revisit this negative view present in the structure of suffering souls. Divisive and negative contemplations must be discerned in their causes and creation.

Of course, what is presented here is the best and highest collection of Orphic ideals, probably not all present in any given period, except in the time of the Master of the Mysteries.

I have seen and been served by such a Master in the form of Avatara Adi Da, the Beloved of my heart, present-time transmitter to anyone who attends to the Truth.

Plato's Inheritance:
A Brief Survey of the Pre-Socratics

It was said by Alfred North Whitehead, and often repeated, that Western philosophy is the footnotes of Plato. The issues he discussed, the broad-mindedness of his critical eye, his height of awe and report of beatitude from his master are the currents throughout the stream of Western thought. So if Western philosophy is the footnotes of Plato, Socrates and the pre-Socrates are his bibliography.

Nietzsche emphasized the depth and magnificence of Socrates and the wisdom tradition that preceded Plato when he boasted that Plato had not one original thought! Therefore let us look at the streams of thought that became confluent in Plato; let us appreciate the philosophers, *physikoi,* theologians, bards, poets, and playwrights before him. If Plato is the Giant, let us appreciate the Titans upon whose shoulders he stood.

Of course, the most significant person in Plato's life was Socrates. It was reported that the aspiring 20 year-old playwright thought he was ready for his first theatre, but had a personal encounter with the Sage of Athens. He went directly home and burned everything he had written. Despite what really smart people say, Socrates was not merely a really smart man. While Socrates' capacity for discrimination and logic went to ground, in some way, he was a simple man, perhaps simpler than anyone else in the Mediterrean. He was stunningly simple in an enlightened way; embarrassingly simple by implication.

Logical Socrates was not just a brilliant man who realized the depth of the mysteries, but like the Orphic realizers, he was imbued with a power of being in communion with what is most real. His strength called upon and imbued this power to others. Socrates was a transmitter, an *Orphetelete*, in addition to knowing nothing at all. Socrates was Plato's world for the ages of twenty to twenty seven. And after Socrates drank his immortal nectar, Plato left Hellas. (For a full visitation of the company of Socrates, please see my book, *The Recollections of Sokrates*.)

Plato spent the next decade in the spiritual community at Krotona, the legacy of Pythagoras.

Plato also went to Egypt and inherited that deep fount of Africa, with their spirituality, their stillness and "fire in the middle" (pyra-mid) knowledge, and contemplated the life of life (zoe vs bios) in their mythologies.

The libraries of Egypt let Plato take in scrolls from the East; he gathered developed Babylonia and mystic India as well. The Hellenes harvested the precepts of the Mediterranean, the steppes of Asia, Middle Earth and marvelous India, and like the Vedanta of India, matured them into concepts.

Intrinsic to the Hellenes, Plato was imbued with the elegance of the Minoans, the Homer-Hesiodic mythologies, and the cosmogony and theology of Orpheus. At home, Plato was an Athenian, absorbing political turmoil, and the genius of that newborn parabola: the theater.

Plato was more than Athenian, he was Hellene, that is, a citizen aligned to Hellas, the province of Delphi and its Oracular sayings. Plato, like everyone who called themselves a Hellene, knew that upon Apollo's Temple at Delphi were the most famous of all maxims: "Know Thyself" and "Nothing in Excess".

Plato was his nickname, Aristekles was his given name and it said that he was once the best wrestler in Athens. Described as broad-shouldered by his coach, the nickname "broad" or "Plato" stuck.

A half century earlier, Socrates was one-year old when Sophocles produced his first play. Socrates' life was a golden time of intellectual and spiritual giants. Herakleitos and Pythagoras had passed away only a generation before, and Parmenides, Zeno, and Empedocles were carrying the mystic torch of the One Being. The Oracle at Delphi was in full power—as were the mysteries of mystic Eleusis and healing Epidavros. The theater was alive with Aeschylus, Sophocles, and Euripides—in a polis where Pericles received the votes of the people and Pindar sang heavenly odes. Hippocrates logically crystallized the medicinal and healing arts of the Asklepians, and Anaxagoras proclaimed the sun was not a god, but a fiery rock ("and probably larger than the

Pelopponese"). Leucippus and Democritus, in devotion to the Master Parmenides, proposed that Being Itself indeed is One and Indestructible, but extremely minute—allowing for movement of the Unmoving, un-split-able One, the a-toms (un-split-able) which make every (seemingly) different thing. All of this, and more, was flourishing aloud in the generation of Socrates—it was the "sixties" of the ancient world.

Into this golden age, brilliant Aristekles was born and matured. As Plato, he witnessed the Hellenic miracle and watched it pass. And he saved all that was before him with an embrace and complexity that matched the magnificence of his inheritance.

Plato's mindful climax unified and preserved the brilliant thoughts of Socrates as well as the Ionians, the Eleatics, and the Athenians. Therefore, let us look in detail at the landscape between Plato and Orpheus, between Italy and Asia Minor, between theology and philosophy.

*****

Science, theology, philosophy, and metaphysics find common ground in *physis*. Usually translated through the Latin *natura* or "nature," *physis* is a extremely broad word and deserves to remain un-translated. Commonly, *physis* has been used in to describe "things", like the natural or physical world. This would, of course, include "physics" and "physical". But *physis* has an etymological, theological, and philosophical essence that is best described as a "blossoming emergence" (Heidegger) which appears, lingers, and passes away. Indeed, before the word "philosopher", humans who contemplated the eternal principles were called *physiologoi* and *physikoi* — those attentive to *physis*.

Peri Physis was the title given to pre-Socratic works about reality (usually translated "On Nature"). *Physis* was the stuff of reality, the blossoming emergence everywhere lingering and passing. The common presumption of the ancient Hellenes was that reality itself, *physis*, was a living and divine process — commonly explained through the mythic interpretation. To inquire into this "hylozoism" or "living reality" or *physis* was the obligation of every one who desired to understand and harmonize with it.

Logos, the ancients noted, not only governed *physis*, it was how one understood it. Thus, the Orphic *theologoi* transformed into the *physiologoi*. (Who were later called *physikoi*, and then "philosophers".)

[Plato suggested four ways to apprehend *theos* (or *physis*): by *epagoge*, the inductive scrutiny (think Socrates); by *analogia*, comparisons (think Herakleitos and Pythagoras); by *aphairesis*, or intelligent negatives (like Socrates himself and the "Neti neti" "not this, not this" of the Indian sage -- also in the West, think Parmenides); and by *ekstasis*, or ecstasy (think the mysteries).]

Integrating the inherent, unconditional joy with the conditional was the goal of the great inquirers and lovers of wisdom. And with the power of the formless in form, remarkable persons posited the first form, the arche. To understand the first form, or archetype, was to understand the bridge between heaven and earth, between the formless joy and all the things here upon the earth. But while the *theologoi* cast images in poesy or rhapsody, the *physikoi* spoke mainly in a new style: prose.

*****

Beginning with the prosaic clarity of the Milesians, a rational cosmology began to augment and replace the theological cosmogony. Aristotle's historical view was that prosaic *physis* replaced rhapsodic theology ("and thinking along these lines") with Thales. Thales (~624-546) was the one of the famous "Seven Wise Men" and was given the title, "Sophos" or Sage. He posited water as the arche, the first form at the root of all living reality—prosaically restating a mythological or cosmogonical assessment of the kosmos. This rational positing of a primeval archetype began a stream that has been called the fountainhead of Western thought. But Thales was said to have written nothing, leaving that task to his younger, genius friend, Anaximander.

Anaximander (~610-546) was purported by Themistius to be the first man "bold enough to publish a treatise on the nature of things." Anaximander's appreciation of the arche was not an element such as water, but the *apeiron*, the "not-bounded", the unlimited. This was not a void or gap, but a substantial, living, and open-ended fullness.

Logos and science was born in appreciation of what is most real. Originally science was not different from theology, but was its spiritual fruit.

Anaximander wrote in prose about the nature of reality, arching a bridge between theological rhapsody and beginning science. (Here, in the interest of the academy, let us bear the caveat: most of what we know about all of these characters is through reference and inference of later writers. Certainty of attribution from within these cloudy historical times is at best an educated deduction. However, the oldest fragments we have today of any of the ancient philosophers is a fragment from Anaximander.)

> *Out of that whence all things have their origin, into that they must also pass away according to necessity; for they must pay penalty and be judged for their injustice, according to the ordinance of time.*

Reciprocity explained without mythology. Anaximander was a giant. Arche, genesis, necessity, destiny, justice, ordinance, the *physis* of appearance, lingering, and disappearance, all of these aspects of reality are profound matters. In Anaximander, we can clearly see the influence of Orphic theology with its concerns of necessity, justice, and the unlimited divine Source of all and All.

But Anaximander spoke this Orphic wisdom into prose and followed Thales' example of attempting to translate the metaphysical vision or rapture into the everyday interactions, and show the unitive presence in the logical nature of things.

Still, Anaximander posited *apeiron*, that which is both undefinable and unconditional as the primary substance of each and every thing. Thus we find a communication between two worlds: the deeply sacred and the newly scientific.

We know from many other sources that Anaximander posited a theory of evolution, both of the cosmological and biological variety. "Man was once a fish" is attributed to him, and he was credited as being the first to suggest the world was not sitting on anything, but was suspended in the cosmos by the equi-distance of everything around it. Supposedly, he was the first to make a *geographia*, a map of the earth, and the first to construct a *sphaira*, a sphere. He was the first to attempt to write a full description of all human knowledge. Anaximander's encyclopedias are lost, but much was inherited into later philosophers. Think Bucky Fuller, Darwin, Copernicus, and Aquinas rolled into one. If Aristotle is the father of the sciences, Anaximander is the grandfather. Indeed, Aristotle himself proclaimed that it was clearly Anaximander "who first entered the realm where philosophy and science in their Western forms became possible."

After Thales and Anaximander opened the realm of the scientific, a new body of representation quickly emerged, creating epistemology, linguistics, philosophy, logic, teleology, and science. The differences in representation and the coming to grips with the limits of language, representation, and knowledge occupied an inordinate amount of conversation—especially when the conversation is about a unitive realization.

We think of Anaximander as a "scientist", but he was equally a theologian, a deeply religious man with a mature and penetrating mind. Our mistaking early prosaic speech for profane talk in the early scientists is a common one. It is our common myopia of scientism projected onto the ancients. We focus on their science as if there were not also brilliant theologians and devoted philosophers.

Physis sometimes emphasized what we call physics or science and sometimes metaphysics, but in any case, the reason for the inquiry into the nature of things was for the realization of the unitive principle which makes the cosmos a universe. A tradition of this unitive realization was being carried by the Orphics and their theology as well as the *physiologoi* and their science. The unified field theory has a long tradition.

After Anaximander came the contemporaries, Anaximenes, Xenophanes, the great Pythagoras, and "Obscure" Herakleitos.

Anaximenes, like all the pre-Socratics, wished "to discover a natural explanation of the manifold variety of physical phenomena consistent with a monist view of reality." Anaximenes followed his teacher Anaximander in most ways—differing in his thesis by positing aether as the arche of existence. To this arche, he added the complementary ideas of "rarefication" and "condensation" which affect the arche—thus describing how quantitative changes could produce qualitative ones. Perhaps his greater contribution was his "plain" scientific language. He made Anaximander look poetic.

While famous for his satirical and sharp tongue, Xenophanes was both a scientist and a deeply spiritual man. He criticized Anaximander's position that all stuff has a divine origin as not strong enough in emphasis on the divinity of existence. He countered: the whole universe is divine, without origin, without genesis or destruction. His "One God" made him the spiritual father of all the Eleatic philosophers—according to Plato and Aristotle.

Xenophanes (~570~475!) is often remembered as the man who cast aside mythological and anthropological conceptions of the divine with the brash statement: "Ethiopians imagine their gods as black and snub-nosed, Thracians as blue-eyed and red-haired ... And if oxen and horse or lions had hands, or could draw and fashion works as men do; horses would draw the gods shaped like horses and lions like lions, making the bodies of the gods resemble their own forms."

Xeno is usually translated as "stranger", the root of our xenophobia. But it was a noteworthy appellation of Zeus because every stranger could be a god, could be a holy ghost, even the Bright One before you. *Zeus Xenia* has us consider every stranger first as a blessing, until they prove otherwise. *Phanes* is the Orphic name for the "primal light" of the universe. Thus "Xenophanes" protrays the holy spirit of original light.

Xenophanes was said to gaze at the whole sky and exclaim, "Unity is God, supreme among gods and men, and not like mortals in body or in mind, there is only eternal being, self-evident, absolute in intelligence." He is also further credited with emphasize on self-evidence: "It takes a wise person to recognize a wise person."

He developed an epistemology that emphasized the discernment between true belief and knowledge. His epistemological enquiry then turned upon knowledge itself, until he concluded that you may know many things about something, but not really know what it is. Isness is beyond knowing, even while informing it.

Xenophanes lived to be 95 years of age, writing elegies in hexameter at 92 and singing of the unbroken divinity without genesis or end. We have only a few quotes of others. He is reported to be the first Hellene to explicitly state that he was writing for future generations, dying slightly before Sokrates would be born.

When Xenophanes was twenty five, his home city of Colophon fell to Harpagus the Mede after Cyrus's conquest of Lydia in 546. Loss of liberty drove Xenophanes (and the many of the brightest from Ionia) to southeast Italy to found the great religious and philosophical cities of Elea and Crotona. The shift from Turkey to Italy marked a new phase of the new consciousness. Xenophanes is the acknowledge father of the Eleatics.

About 540, back in the great Asia Minor city of Epheseus, the distant grandson of Androclus (founder and King of the city) was born. He was in line to inherit the first chair and was given every advantage. Most of all, however, young Herakleitos was impressed by the wise man, Hermodorus.

When Hermodorus' truth-telling penetrated the political status-quo, the men of the Epheseus drove Hermodorus out of town. (He went to Rome and assisted in drawing up the laws of the Twelve Tables.) Herakleitos railed, "Every grown man of the Ephesians should hang himself, and leave the city to the boys; for the men banished Hermodorus, the best man among them, saying, 'Let no one of us excel, or if he does, be it elsewhere and among others'."

Herakleitos gave up his aristocracy and inheritance—ceding it to his brother—and renounced the common world. Once, he was found playing dice with children in the streets and the elders of the town reproached him. He answered back, "Why are you surprised, you good-for-nothings? It's better than playing politics with you!"

But Herakleitos' exposure to the wisdom tradition vaulted his inquiry to a radical renunciation. Supposedly, he retreated from Ephesus into the distant hills and lived as a hermit. Like his contemporary Gautama to the East, Herakleitos gave himself to a life of contemplation. "I sought my true self."

Coming to a fundamental understanding, he supposedly wrote a treatise on *Physis*, and left it one day at the Temple of Artemis in the city's center. We have fragments, mainly from others' recitations. "Fools are those who are not in constant intercourse with their own divine nature. You cannot step twice into the same river. Human nature has no true insight, but rather the divine nature has it. The way up and down is one and the same..."

Instead of the new dialectic style of prose, Herakleitos deliberately spoke in the ancient style of prophetic maxims as he compared reality (*physis*) to an eternal fire, governed by *logos* and understood by the same.

Logos is the harmonic gathering of opposites, the resolution of paradoxes, common to all and universal, ever-lasting, all-pervading, governing all movement. Logos is comprehended best by the open mind and relaxed consciousness wherein all things appear naturally.

Herakleitos: "God is day night, winter summer, war peace, satiety hunger; things taken together are wholes and not whole, something which is being brought together and brought apart, which is in tune and out of tune; out of all things there comes a unity, and out of a unity all things."

"For, though all things come to pass in accordance with this *Logos*, men seem ignorant when they experience such words and things as I set forth, distinguishing each thing according to it nature and tell how it is. Although this *Logos* is as I describe, men prove as unable to understand it when they hear it as before they hear it. Though the *Logos* is common to all, men live as if they had a private understanding of their own. They do not apprehend how being at variance it agrees with itself; there is a back-stretched connexion, as in the bow and the lyre."

Herakleitos' embrace of the contradictions was brilliant beyond any previous conception. Only intellectual giants understood him and Plato loved him. Herakleitos' thesis that *logos* governed and understood *physis* blended the wise mind into the source Brightness (Zeus). As Heraklitos must have said with a smile, "The Wise is One Only, it does and does not consent to be called by the name, "Zeus" "If you have not heard me by all of this but the Logos, then I can say, All is One." This unitive logos also was not lost on broad Plato.

Pantoi Rhei, "Everything Flows". Herakleitos' thesis that the kosmos was "an ever living fire, which is being kindled in measures and extinguished in measure, but it always was and is and shall be" has taken on renewed relevance in the last century. In the 1950's, Heisenberg wrote extensively on the Fire of Herakleitos in the light of modern physics, suggesting Herakleitos put forth the first principles of physics with founding force.

Herakleitos' psychological wisdom found in two fragments must be reviewed, even in a survey such as this. The first is *ethos anthropos daimon,* usually translated as "A man's character is his fate." More than suggesting a godless relationship between personality and destiny, the entire Orphic cosmogony about the Fates, one's *daimon,* and Necessity are summarized in prophetic prose. An in-depth study of *ethos* and *anthropos* and *daimon* reveals a fuller translation: "The spirit who guides me is myself as I authentically am."

Authenticity exceeds the "Spindle destiny", exceeds all the threads that make up the fabric of one's life. One ceases to be subject to the stars or mother, father, or culture. Herakleitos: "Do not be the child of your mother and father", suggesting a maturity that is not-dependent, non-passive, and non-subjective, but rather interdependent, receptive and responsive, being authentic. Herakleitos remains a fount of wisdom that needs to be drunk every generation.

But for the most part, "after the Medes", the Ionian brilliance went west to Italy, especially upon the mantle of Xenophanes, where new colonies could live freely outside of tyranny.

Pythagoras was born about 570 and was clearly influenced by the Indian-inspired Orphic teachings and mysteries. To argue the One was not his passion, his was to personally realize the harmonies of that mystic divinity, understand it even mathematically, and teach others to reap the fruits of divine devotion and enlightened understanding. Therefore, he did not found just a philosophical school, but a religious community, more like an ashram than a monastery. And finally, through the school of Pythagoras, women were received as equal.

We commonly remember Pythagoras for "the square of the sides equals the square of the hypotenuse" and for his discovery of the mathematical relationships in music. But Pythagoras was unabashedly religious in intent, even as he made significant mathematical and harmonic advances amidst the "ashram" atmosphere at Crotona. Instead of positing a substance at the origin of things, Pythagoras' thesis was that mathematical relationships were the key to understanding. So potent were his findings and assertions that over entrance to Plato's Academy in Athens were the words, "Let no one enter here who is not a student of geometry."

So powerful was the religious impact of Pythagoras, mystic knowledge after him came to be described as "Pythagorean-Orphic". He confessed that he was not wise about *physis*, but was a "lover of wisdom". Thus Pythagoras was the first to be called a "philosopher". Much could be said about his religious teachings, his community, his life, and his lineage. For now, let us state that Pythagoras was a powerful force in the mind of Plato, who first went to Crotona after the death of Socrates. Therefore, let us follow Pythagoras' direct lineage through an obscure devotee, "a poor man of fine character," Ameinias.

Ameinias is not important to us for what he taught but whom. He passed on the mystic embrace of the Living One that he had received from Pythagoras to a student of Xenophanes, a giant named Parmenides. In an age where attribution of lineage was all-important, Parmenides built a temple to Ameinias upon his death. In Parmenides, we have the "One God" of Xenophanes together with the transmission of mystic realization from Pythagoras.

Parmenides (~515~406) rocked the free world, not by positing the perfect arche or datum's origin, but by asking "What is Truth and how is it different from Illusion and the world of appearances? What is Is? What is Being?" In Parmenides we again find the comparison of the aesthetic against the nous, the trust in reason over trust in the senses, the seniority and superiority of *noeton* (consciousness) over *aistheton* (appearances), and how the datum of the eyes and ears is given to dreamy illusion and how the *logos* awakens one to the Real.

Plato called Parmenides "a reverend and awe-filled figure" and it was told that the elder Parmenides inspired young ten-year-old Socrates. While his personal presence was certainly an initiation (*telete*) into the feeling of unitive consciousness, his words have lasted. By the gods, we have much of his famous poem, written in hexameter metre, the style of Homer and Xenophanes.

In the metaphorical poem, the Truth (*Aletheia*) is a goddess (*thea*) who calls Parmenides to look (*thea*) at the differences between appearances and the truth. He experience the differences between the opinions of mortals and the formless joy of inherent being. Heidegger's translations have always moved me: "It is necessary for you (who are now entering on the path to being) to experience everything, the untrembling heart of well-rounded unconcealment (aletheia) as well as the views of men, in which there dwells no reliance of the unconcealed... But only the legend remains of the Way; how it stands with being; on this (way) there are many indications: how being, without genesis, is without destruction, complete, alone there without tremor and not still requiring to be finished; nor was it before, nor will it be in the future, for being present it is entirely, unique, unifying, united, gathering itself in itself from itself (cohesive, full of presentness)."

"Come, I will tell you: heed well the words that you hear (as to) which ways of inquiring are along to be considered. The one: how it is (how being is) and how non-being is impossible. This is the path of justified confidence, for it follows unconcealment (*aletheia*), the Truth."

Looking (*thea*) where the goddess (*thea*) of Truth pointed, Parmenides journeyed though the Night by Stillness until the Day, and saw the revelation and merged into the Truth beyond the opinion mind of mortals. By following Truth, we pass through the many dualisms to the One Being; we go beyond temporal considerations of Becoming and motion to presently practicing the unchanging truth of real existence.

That reality is the always new One, fresh life, being, heart-light, instrinsic awareness, *nous;* where even "Apprehension and being are the same."

"This metaphysical concept of immutable being, and the epistemological contention that knowledge is only explicable as a contact of the mind with an actual stable and non-sensible object of knowledge, are cornerstones of Plato." Indeed, in his Timeaus (27d), we read pure Parmenides: "In my opinion we must first of all make the following distinction: what is it that always is and has no becoming, and what on the other hand becomes continually and never is? The one comprehensible by the mind with reasoning, the other conjectured by opinion with irrational sensation, coming to be and passing away, but never really being. But it now is, all together, one and continuous. It is and always was and always shall be." !!

Parmenides is said to have nurtured all the Eleatics and philosophy proceeded as angles upon his absolute standing in unchanging, free being. In defense of Parmenides and his supporters, the proclamation of One Being is worth the loudest of trumpets. His presence was strong, and, by legend and report, awesome. However, there is a problem with Parmenides' ideal of the eternal Unity as unmoving, unchanging, and indivisible: a problem that came to be called, "saving the phenomena". Into this solution stepped the last "pre-Socratic" figures in our survey.

Zeno (490-?), a contemporary of Anaxagoras, was a disciple/student of Parmenides and took up the shout of unitive vision. He spoke his *logoi*, his arguments, in terms of hypothesis versus hypothesis, not only arguing his point, but also making parody of the limitations of conventional mind. His compelling koans and playful paradoxes were logical devices to support his master's adamant defense of the One unmoving Being that Is Truth and Consciousness. Zeno's arrow never reaches the target because the usual mind locates the flying arrow in Becoming. This critique of conventional thinking supported his teacher's One Being.

Other pillars on the temple of Plato's mind were Empedocles (492-432), the scientist and mystic, the one who personified the union of rational thought with mystical exaltation, applying his spiritual power to philosophy, mysticism, medicine, politics, and poetry, showing (off) how a higher intelligence can flow into different fields. Indeed, Aristotle held his words in such high regard that he credited Empedocles with the invention of the art of rhetoric. He too tried to "save the phenomena", attempting to unite Being and

Becoming. "In some way, things do come to be and perish, in another they are for ever."

Empedocles was most highly regarded for his "man of all worlds" personae. That he could be a most outrageous Orphic mystic and Eleatic philosopher and equally powerful in medicine and politics made him a giant in the minds of those who knew of him. He was a divine man to thousands. Indeed, his entrance into cities was often filled with flower petals and celebration.

"Friends, I bid you hail. I an immortal god, no longer a mortal, go about among you all, honored as is proper for me, crowned with fillets and blooming garlands. When I come to flourishing cities, I am an object of reverence to men and women. They follow me in their thousands, asking whither leads the way to profit, some desiring oracles, whereas others seek to hear the word of healing for every kind of disease, long time transfixed by sore anguish."

"Friends, I know that the truth is in the words which I shall speak, but hard and painful is the entry of understanding into the minds of men."

Empedocles' cure for the "saving the phenomena" was to see the One in terms of primary psychology: Love and Strife. The lens of strife saw the duplicity of the world, whereas love intimated the One. While the gradual transformation of the seer into the philosopher had begun with Anaximander, in Empedocles both worlds were at their acme. He was a multi-peaked mountain.

In contrast to the mystic idealism of passionate Empedocles was the mindful realism of calm Anaxagoras (500?-428BCE). Like Herakleitos, he gave up political and social power along with extensive wealth to lead a contemplative life, *theoria metaphysikoi kai physikoi,* "contemplating philosophy and how things come into being." When reproached for neglect to his fatherland, Anaxagoras is said to have replied, "You are wrong, I do indeed care for my fatherland," as he pointed and looked heavenward.

The following of Anaxagoras was wide and amongst his closest students were Euripides, Pericles, and, most imporantly, Archelaus (teacher of Socrates). Like Anaximander, Anaxagoras was a genius of perspective, and according to Plutarch, he "produced the first and clearest explanation in writing of the illumination and shadow of the moon"; and by Hippolytus, he "figured the sizes and distances of the sun and moon and recognized the marks on the moon as shadows caused by mountains."

Anaxagoras addressed the One of Parmenides by identifying things with becoming and being with *Nous*. "There is a wrong conception of becoming and perishing. Nothing comes to be or perishes, but there is mixture and separation of things that exist. They ought properly call generation 'mixture' and extinction 'separation'... The rest have portion of everything, but Mind/Intelligence (*Nous*) is something infinite and not dependent, and is mixed with no thing, but alone and by itself. Awareness sets everything in order... There are many portions of many things, and no one thing is completely separated or divided from another save *Nous*. *Nous* is all alike, both the greater and the smaller... the finest and purest of all things, and has all knowledge of everything and greatest power." Instead of debating "philosophical" theory, Anaxagoras was known for bringing the discussion to the efficacy of wisdom over folly. A-theistic consciousness instead of an objective, emanative divinity was the emphasis of Anaxagoras.

Anaxagoras, like Galileo, is known for being charged with denying the divinity of heavenly bodies. When Anaxagoras proclaimed "The sun is not a god, but a burning rock, and it's probably larger than the Peloponnese," he was brought before the religious authorities of Athens and charged with impiety. Anaxagoras chose exile over hemlock, as was the custom. (Young Socrates saw it all.)

Anaxagoras' pupil, Archelaus, "the physicist", continued the *archai* of Anaxagoras, *Nous*, Consciousness. He argued that right and wrong were not absolutes of deities, but conventions of human ideas. He is said to have pioneered the antithesis between nature and convention. With thought such as this, being human began to replace the kosmos as the focus of interest. Human interest began to take center stage; the anthroposphere had begun. Archelaus was the personal teacher to Socrates, since Anaxagoras had declined the hemlock.

Contemporary Democritus is associated mostly with the creation of atomic theory. He is said to have created vast volumes on many sciences, and was compared in this accomplishment to Aristotle. Unfortunately, none have survived. Democritus also tried to "save the phenomena" by agreeing with Parmenides that Being indeed in One and indivisible— but composed of extremely minute, uniform particles that were indeed "in-divisible", the *a-tom*. While we think of Democritus as if he were an empirical scientist with an electron microscope, he too was a sacred physicist, arguing for the unitive vision that makes the kosmos a universe.

Diogenes, "the natural philosopher", of Apollonia (formerly known as *Eleuthernae*) proposed that the origin of all things was air, but not air as we think of it, but of conscious space, divine intelligence. Or as he plainly wrote, "And I hold that that which has intelligence is what men call air. All men are guided by it, and it masters all things. I hold that this Same is Divine, and that it reaches everything and disposes all things and is in everything."

All of these giants, along with Aeschylus, Sophocles, Euripides, and Pericles affected Plato, and were personae, arguments, and revelations to whom he would have to answer and incorporate, along with the mysteries and Orphic Initiators of spiritual force.

Let it be stated that those mentioned in this brief survey of Plato's inheritance were not yet crippled by the chronic doubt of modernity, and so all contemplated (*theoria*) their view (*thesis*) to encompass the entire universe and the divinity (*theion*) of its nature. Chronic doubt eventually occluded the Real One in an insubstantial deconstruction, assigning the divinity of reality to the sentiments of a subjectivist projecting illusions into a world of things.

Sokrates put out a warning to the subjectivists: "If you look at the world only through materialist eyes, you'll be like those who gaze upon the eclipse and go blind. You must not forgo tending to your feeling-being; you must attend to your soul."

Unlike all truth-tellers before him charged with impiety, Sokrates did not go elsewhere. He called their bluff. He knew the hemlock would be ambrosial.

As we make a rational reconstruction of the trans-rational spectrum of illumination, we may once again appreciate and marvel at the sacred work of the early *physilogoi*, reintegrate the awe and clarity of the pre-Socratics, Socrates, and Plato, and let all things and thoughts rest in and as One Brightness.

Have you heard? Energy equals matter times the speed of light squared.

Everybody here is like an archeological site,
a place where archaeologists dig through the ground,
finding towns and specimens of history
(biological or animal or human cultural history)
in strata, in layers.
Every human being is like such a site,
because we do not live in an initiatory culture.
Each of us is possessed of very complex subjectivity
that is made of archaic moments of adaptation.
When we are confronted by the circumstances of life,
we resort, at random, very primitively
and very automatically to these solutions.
Any of the strata of old adaptation
can come to light at any time —
and that is our liability in the world.
We must reach a point in our living,
in our initiation into life,
where we no longer resort to these archaisms.
We have a pristine or prior responsibility to love,
to remain in communication—
in other words, to live this *moment*
rather an archaic one.

—Avatara Adi Da Samraj (Eleutherios)

An Ecstatic Appreciation of History
and This Moment in Time

"Each of us is like an archeological site, with layers or strata of history that can be felt in our own body-mind." Thus Adi Da Eleutherios describes in a personal way how the developmental stages and nuances of an individual can be seen in social and evolutionary history. This is usually summarized as "ontogeny recapitulates phylogeny," for indeed there are parallels in stage and lesson along personal and social developmental lines. With stage and lesson clarified, we may gracefully arrive in our historical moment with an elegant willingness.

This Eleutherian wisdom also tells us that the individual not only summarizes history, but likened unto an archeological dig, there is a truthful process of responsibility whereby we bring what is dark, un-conscious, and limited into the light of consciousness — thus allowing feeling to pass beyond previous limits. This is a process of feeling and seeing previous adaptations, and then understanding them. By such acceptance, understanding, and empowered by new adaptations, feeling can become free and the truth can be directly felt. Such is the heroic journey through the underworld and the ordinary way of growing up and arriving responsively in this moment.

To elucidate history in this way is not about information and facts, but rather a way to talk about our essential responsibility. Hopefully, this will throw light onto our historical moment as we arrive at the present truth of a single human family in need.

We do this unfolding work most personally. Rather than being fixed in anxious habits, our moral obligation empowers us to be able to clearly respond and serve, beyond any occluded reaction. This response-ability is the capacity this conversation attempts to serve, using history as one canvas upon which to view an archeological picture of man and woman. Coming at last to the present, our moment in time and responsibility is clarified.

I speak as a Westerner, as Hellene. I speak in terms of Beauty, Pathos, Love, Truth, Reality, and Ecstasy. But more than Hellene, I am human. In a very large family.

It behooves everyone to revisit the sacred origins of our thought, revisiting not only our idealistic mythology, but the *mysteria* and original *theologoi* that blossomed as realistic *philosophia*. Indeed, Socrates himself validated true *philosophia* as being the same as the true realizers of the mysteries (and he lampooned the fakes). Now we are lost in naive realism and the flatland of the thinking mind, and it behooves us to re-inherit the foundational clarity and depth of feeling from our rich origins. *A-peras,* the un-limited, is how the great Anaximander prosaically described the core of everything. (Then Socrates claimed not-knowing.)

There is little written about Delphi or Orpheus that is anything more than the superficial, exoteric, and conventionally believable high-school-book-report point of view. This is understandable. The true religious and spiritual process has been abstracted and "believed" out our common Western culture by conventional science and conventional religion. This seems to be slowly changing. *The View from Delphi* joins an expression of a regeneration of a view whose prominence for the last two thousand years has been dwindled close to nil by our scientistic, materialistic hyper-individuality, but truly can been never lost.

For half a century, I have been dedicated to uncovering of what is meant by religious and spiritual endeavors. I practice an esoteric teaching under the guidance of Adi Da Eleutherios in which my critical understanding of the Great Tradition of humanity's religious and spiritual paths, both ancient and modern, is combined with full bodily and feeling practices of divine intimacy. Like the Sibyl of the Oracle, I speak from experience on what it is to be possessed by a god.

Deep in heart-joy, every memory of everyone and every animal dissolves. Undone by divinity received, vast knowledge flashes in the heart, just before the formless joy. In Orphic lore, this was known as *The Book of the Muses*. The Hindus used a Sanskrit term *akashic* (lit. "sky") to refer a kind of memory, or rather remembrance and consciousness, that is intrinsic, cellular, instinctive, psychic. Libraries of knowledge can be reflected from this heart sky. These "akashic" gifts, combined with a few historical verifications and native impulse to share brings this book of musings to you. I pray you enjoy it.

For water was the origin for the totality of things, according to him [Orpheus], and from water slime was established, and from both of them was generated a living creature, a snake with a lion's head growing on to it, and in the middle of them the face of a god, Heracles and Chronos by name. This Heracles generated a huge egg, which being completely filled by the force of its begetter burst into two through friction. So its top part was the sky Ouranos, and the underneath Gaia.

— Athenagoras

Verily first did Chaos come into being, and then the broad bosomed Gaia, a firm seat of all things forever, and misty Tartaros in a recess of broad-wayed earth, and Eros, who is fairest among immortal gods, looser of limbs, and subdues in their breasts the mind and gives thoughtful counsel to all gods and all men.

And Earth first of all brought forth the starry sky, equal to herself, to cover her completely about, to be a firm seat for the blessed gods forever.

—Hesiod, Theogony 116

From the Beginning...

For billions of years life has organically grown, evolved, and followed its own pattern of brightness here on this blue-green planet. Man and woman have been a relative new comers to this process and, as a form of Life, contain all that is before them. In the words of Eleutherios,

> *If the design of Man is examined, he is revealed to be a composite of all previous creatures, environments, and experiences. His body below the brows is a machine of animals and elemental cycles. He is full-made of horses and crocodiles, honey bees and swans, sardines and earth forces, redwood and fruit palm, Amazon, Pacific, solar fire, Everest, weather of water and air, all the usual stars, and antique ocean mammals leaning away from Earth.*

It is useful to feel and understand all that we were and are. To engage this feeling-understanding is always a *present* process, a revelatory process whereby our capacity to feel is strengthened and grows to freedom. As the crown of creation and the basis for thought, feeling-attention is the continuation of the sizzling brightness that is life itself, in and as each of us.

The uncovering, feeling into and through what is presently the habitual unconscious animal and elemental aspect of ourselves certainly captures a great deal of our attention. To stand free in that, as that, and then of that animal and elemental un-consciousness is no longer a heroic possibility, but our human responsibility.

This process of allowing, freedom, and conscious being also has historical occasions. Great, truly great, men and women throughout the history of our conversation have spoken and shouted about this responsibility and possibility. Irresponsible men and women have kindly turned a deaf ear or else crucified the bright voice in the animal of their choice.

Looking back and inheriting vast eons, we enquire: How did animals and humankind come to evolve from merely organic and lively matter? And looking at the most advanced hominds, we naturally ask, What is it to be human? What is it to be a man or a woman and not merely a male nor female animal?

Visualize a rich organic soup becoming more and more refined, more and more sensitive, evolving into subtlety and complexity within the infinite life field for billions of years as a numinous awareness grew continuously. By the time of the hominids this awareness was providing for the harmonizing experience, developing tools, cooperating with others, tending fires then starting them, until the *conscious contemplation of death bolted awareness to self-reflection,* and thus man and woman to fundamental knowledge and consequent language. Having tasted the deadly fruit of the tree of knowledge, man and woman, as man and woman, stepped from the ocean of living energy even as we are always only simultaneous with it. Death different from embedded life is the origin of understanding. Knowledge of the limit of death defines us exactly. The awareness of mortality reflected a thunderbolt in the dark sky, sparking being in primordial man and woman. I die, therefore I am.

fire tender

I was the fire tender, before knowing
with a mind of a small child,
like every other fascinating thing
I noticed the changes in the moon and the seasons
the rise and fall, the rise and fall.

From snake and cats and tree-climbers I came;
and tended the volcanic and lightning fires
until I could spark one.
At last, I noticed death itself
and the knowledge of good and fear.

Naming, language, and speech were born
from the intelligent womb of primordial sounds,
starting with me and stretching across the millennia
reaching to you and the good, forward and before.
I began counting moons, sparking fires, and thinking,
thinking

Until there is understanding, the tension
of me and everything else is
the same as the tension of time;
past tense, future tense, present tense
happening to me.

Until there is understanding, I am wandering
from the garden of ignorance and myth
beyond facts and mere knowledge
toward a future and mysterious time,
where the freeing of feeling empowers a radical
responsibility
and the nameless understanding recaptures the child
as the tension of time is un-done in a fiery presence

What *is* the primary definition of humans? What is it that truly separates us humans, defines us, different from all that is before us? It is this *discretion* between life and death. While other higher animals know that an intimate has died, the symbology that would sign the explicit knowledge of self-death is apparently absent in all but us. The definition of humanity begins with this living knowledge of our own death. This polar ratio and primal discretion creates the radius of circumspection, the rational means, and later plumbs the depth of radical understanding.

Self-awareness arises from the attention to self-death, but this true recognition of death gives sign to another aspect of awareness. Life and *pathos* suddenly stand out brighter than before: such is the foundation of explicit friendship, civility, and the adoration of beauty.

Civil-ization is the acculturation of this awareness of awe-filled life, of life beyond the limitations of flesh and self. Upon the sobriety of mortality, the balance of *dike,* justice, makes the laws. Upon the mutual acknowledgement of death, *city* states, states of civility acculture the citizens to consider the eternal life wherein the personal life arises and passes, and thus live in harmony.

Civil. What does this word signify? The deepest etymological roots of civil is the Sanskrit *siva. Siva* is the Indian name of the primary god of both pure consciousness and death. *Si* can be heard in dissolve, hiss, snake, silent, and *va* can be found in voice, voluntary, vote, vow. *Si-va.* The awareness of self-dissolution is spontenously followed by the voice of self-awareness. Si-va, Siva, civil, cities, citizen. We die; we are citizens.

Prior to man and woman and therefore to a *very* high degree in us, Life's impulse had been preoccupied with vital satiation. Beauty and delight seemed to be moments in the eye of the storm of survival. While awareness in most animals feels the inherent joy of fundamental awareness, there is no life and death pole of self-reflection. Thus for animals, there was no release but only temporary relief, momentary satisfaction. The onliness of all-pervading life provides much relief from this struggle of incarnation, but without self-consciousness, relief does not even begin to morph into release.

Numenous-ness vaulted past the slower genetic march by the awareness of mortality as word-sounds became discrete communication. Man and woman began their naming, stepping from the garden of nature into the adventure of consciousness.

The word *man* itself is in the same group of sounds as moon, month, measure, ma, me, and in Hindi *maya*, (illusion). Man is the measure of all things, Protagoras noted. Likewise, Adam and Eve named all creatures and creations.

Thus, man and woman began the toil of apprehension, of uncovering, or bringing all that was before them, both in space and in time, into the light of understanding. In discovery, myth, law, and full in truth, that urge is native to us, and always has been.

As unique as every individual is, each of us is also identical to the life-form that has been here for billions of years. In the fabric of shared feeling, we have eaten and been eaten, killed and been killed, used and been used, robbed nests and graves, mothered and fathered, sobbed and sang, resisted and accepted a million deaths. We have been random and specific; lived with frustration, temporary satisfactions, and inherent pleasure. As Life, you and I have lived in wonder, helplessness, and most recently, in knowledge.

Through the process of apprehending what we are historically, life's growth as consciousness continues, and it serves this process whereby we happily become coincident with Life itself, feeling everything freely. With our perturbances seen and released, and as new adaptations harmonize the life, our awareness is found in the ground of being itself. This process is told in a thousand religious stories, often including this "return" or archeological passage to the source of life. The aspirant goes through what is un-seen, *hades,* or the fearful obstruction to joy. Such was *gnosis:* divine knowledge while alive, useful knowledge after death.

Spectra of Maturations and the Existence Place

The "return" or archeological/psychological passage through the underworld journeys through our previous adaptations. By such ground-turning work, we plow new fields of enjoyment as we grow in self-understanding. We uncover and see, feel into, and then understand old patterns; thus we can choose new ones, usually slowy.

The patterns of individual development and the patterns of social development are obviously interrelated. Therefore to rightly understand history one must have a mature comprehension of the subtleties and nuances of human possibility, including its Fullness.

Our Great Tradition of Wisdom gives us a host of developmental possibilities and accountabilities. From the *samadhi, moksha,* and *nirvana* of India to the "sustained ecstasy," "self-realization," and "eternal celebration" of the Orphics, we find similarities. These heavenly universals can be found in every culture, land, and religion and are obviously prior to the differences of each province.

A universal and nuanced understanding of the developmental process is required, one that understands not only the ability of each phase, but the myopia of each stage, and how each step of development has crucial impact in personal and historical archetypes.

Not to repeat or elaborate on what has been done well, let me recommend two books by Ken Wilber: *Up from Eden* (brilliantly delineates both the personal and historical), and *Integral Psychology*, (true to its name, it integrates a multitude of pschological and spiritual frameworks, including Adi Da's.)

From the back cover of *Up from Eden (1986)*:

Beginning with the archaic world, primitive in its beliefs and practices, it moves to the stage of magic — rituals, totems, and struggle for life and death in a world of participation mystique. The next step is the mythic world — the great classical civilizations of the world's enduring mythologies, magnificent in their expression, but hiding a dark side of human sacrifice and ritual immolation. And finally we reach the present stage of rationality, brilliant in its logic, but alienated from its past organic roots, scarred by a repression of the body by the mind.

Magical, mythic, and rational have characterized most of our appreciations world-wide. The limitations of the magical and mythical frameworks in a modern world are lampooned by the rational mind — and we have seen how the mythic can react to such humor with terror.

But however immature mythic thinking can be, the rational limitations are not as clear to the rational mind, naturally. So let us feather this out, and as an added benefit, perhaps we can help restore better relations with the mythic and provincial minds.

One point in the process of maturation is critical: the transition from adolescent to adult. The clarity we gain about this transition can serve the historical crisis we are in with a necessary elegance.

The herald of the rational mind, "science", is rooted in the Latin *scio*, "I know". Its deepest root is in *skei*, "to cut, to split"; this cutting/splitting is well illustrated by an etymological cousin of "science": "shed". When you build a shed roof, it makes a cut in the rain, splitting off a discrete patch of dryness.

Splitting something off to hold it for a view yields vast treasures of knowledge, beginning with a dry place to sleep. But the shed of science has an infamous dark side with shadows in separativeness, lack of feeling, and alienation. And from the separative position, we manipulate the world in abstraction through masks we barely see.

The appreciation of maturation greater than myth and science is not a "philosophic" enterprise, juggling big ideas for their own sake, but rather one that serves the discrimination that clarifies our responsibility to emerge from the separative prison of mentality and the fiery cave of adolescence. Such immaturity is suffocating and killing us.

We must accelerate the conversion from the scientific and rational to the whole, from identification with the internal thinking stream to mutuality in relationship and gratitude in reality. This transition of the adolescent to true adulthood is the transition from the cave of manipulation to lighted interdependence. It is the beginning of adult responsibility and societal fullness.

This critical transition in human development corresponds to our social crisis and historical moment. We are emerging from manipulative and aggressive epochs on the world stage and it is crucial we understand what is required to mature beyond manipulative frameworks and so accelerate this change to cooperation. Otherwise, we increase the coming pain.

Our present moment in history is crucial. Even a bit more responsibility will bypass great suffering. The flying-at-us challenges at the global scale, teetering here and there on collapse and natural horrors are threatening a cascade of dark ages.

What is it that we need to know? What don't we know about the transition from adolescence to adulthood?

First let me say, no one has ever really grown up because it was a good idea. This transition is not one blossom replacing another or an easy morphing of one stage to the next (as does happen). The transition from adolscent to adult is rather a radical conversion that requires explicit self-knowledge and the recognition of self-created pain, (*dukkha* in Pali). Indeed, this is the first noble truth. To mature beyond mentality and the pains of abstraction, we must acutely suffer our own form of Narcissus, see our own self-possessions. Only thus do we *repent* (lit. turn from pain) of the pain we cause; we turn from our self-orientation to giving in relationship. Of course, habits persist and so in understanding, we cleave to relationship; we submit to responsibility, more and more.

We grow beyond the accomplishments of adolescence, science, and rationality, and yield to the fullness that already surrounds us. This maturity is not something we achieve, it is found in giving and receiving, not getting and succeeding.

We learn to offer our position and yield to the council of all. We learn not only to focus with a will, but willingly surrender. Not only do we personally grow, we must grow beyond the independent nation-states mentality and live interdependently in one world as a single human family.

The key in the transition to real adulthood is that the pain our selfishness creates is "shoved back in our face." How much shit in our face will it take before self-understanding enables our hearty embrace of relationship? How bitter and violent will the waters and airs get before we change our manipulative angles into the well-rounded whole? How much suffering will be necessary for everybody all at once to declare that competition for resources, dominance, and war is over? How dark will it get if we fail to heed the call?

Fortunately, each of us already stands in the very place that affects everything: I am. Our very being is the same being that blossoms every where. We can feel this most directly: our practice of care radiates to the whole world. Our practice of service gets passed forward. Our breaths reach far. Our recognition of our single human family is spreading. Be a voice for This.

Before Abraham was, I am. As we stand in the only place we really are, mountains will move. Breathe deeply, feel thoroughly, find the voices who are awake and awakening, and adapt to a new world of real adults.

References

Avatara Adi Da (1978) *The Enlightenment of the Whole Body,* Clearlake, California, The Dawn Horse Press. This is the book that "enlightened" Ken Wilber for its penetrating descriptions of the religious, mystic, and causal dimensions of human potentiality. *The Enlightenment of the Whole Body* describes in depth the "esoteric anatomy" of the mystic as well as the causal seat of human identity in twentieth century language using the medical anatomy of scientific analysis. (On the proverbial island, this is the book I save for future generations.) *Crazy Da Must Sing* (1983)*, Conscious Exercise and the Transcendental Sun* (1976), *Do You Know What Anything Is?* (1984)

W.K.C.Guthrie. (1952) *Orpheus and Greek Religion,* Princeton, New Jersey, Princeton Press. This book is the central text for all scholarly works on Orphism. Guthrie covers Orphism across several centuries and goes into detail about every feature of Orphism. It is thoroughly researched and cross-referenced with Plato, Aristotle, and

numerous ancient philosophers.
*A History of Greek Philosophy. Volume I,
The earlier Presocratics and the
Pythagoreans,* Cambridge Universtity Press,
Cambridge, Mass (Vol 1); (1965)
*A History of Greek Philosophy. Volume II,
The Presocratics Tradition from Parmenides
to Democritus,* Cambridge Universtity Press,
Cambridge, Mass (Vol 2)

G.R.S. Mead. Kessinger Press, *Orpheus*. Mead
was Madame Blavaksy's personal
secretary and a scholar in his own right.
The research and source materials in
this book are quite rich and ranks with
Guthrie's book.

Erwin Rohde (1925), *Psyche*, Chicago, Illinois,
Ares Press. In Orphism, the "psyche" as
we know it first came into being. Rohde's
book, *Psyche,* covers the origins and
manifestations of *psyche* throughout the
ancient world. Meticulously researched,
each chapter ends with many pages of
rich footnotes. Of course, Orphism and
the ancient religious figures are
prominent. The book is subtitled, "The
Belief in Souls and the Cult of
Immortality," which are primary Orphic

themes.

Edinger, Edward F. (1999), *The Psyche in Antiquity*. Inner City Books. Brilliant, and especially illuminating the nuances of the key word *physis.*

William Greene (1948) *Morai: Fate, Good, and Evil in Greek Thought*, Cambridge, Massachusetts, Harvard Univerity Press. This is another seminal and classic treatise on early Greek thought. How the early Westerners accounted for reciprocity within the contexts of time and character was commonly understood by the "spindle destiny" of necessity and the fates. These were Orphic constructions, and Greene communicates the compelling arguments of destiny and reciprocity with clarity.

Plato: (The Four Dialogues: Phaedrus, Phaedo, Symposium, Timeaus) from *The Collected Dialogues of Plato*, Edited by Edith Hamilton and Huyntington Cairns, Bollingen Series, Princeton University Press, 1961/rev.89

F.E.Peters, *Greek Philosophical Terms*, New York University Press, New York. This historical lexicon traces the implications of each philosophical term through time. Greek literary and philosophical examples from different times and men give unique insight into the depth of the word.

Martin Heidegger, 1959, *Introduction to Metaphysics*, Yale University Press, London. "Introduction" indeed. Here Heidegger dives into a few fragments of the ancients with uncommon etymological depth. (Read it every year for a couple of decades.) Excellent for depth in the thinking of Parmenides and Herakleitos. *Early Greek Thinking*, (1975), (EGT) Harper and Row, New York

Peter Kingsley, 1990. *Wisdom in Dark Places*, Cambridge Press, Cambridge. A re-examination of the life of Parmenides and the Orphic roots of his mysticism. Excellent for its insights of resting in the darkness, "like an animal in its lair."

The Mysteries, Edited by Joseph Campbell. 1955. Princeton University Press, Princeton, N.J. Joseph Campbell knows how to find great writings on the religious phenomena called "the mysteries." Particular strength by Walter Wili on the Orphic mysteries.

Walter Burkert, 1990. *Greek Religion*, Harvard University Press. Another highly respected and well-written book on Hellenic mythology, theology, spirituality, and philosophy.

G.S. Kirk, J.E. Raven and M. Schofield (1957) *The Pre-Socratics,* Cambridge Universtity Press, Cambridge, Mass

Clifford H Moore, 1916 *The Religious Thought of the Greeks*, Cambridge Harvard University Press, Oxford

Will Durant, 1939. *The Life of Greece*, Simon and Shuster, New York. If you want an excellent survey on the philosophical, political life of the ancient Hellene as well as a detailed description of every day life, this is the classic reference.

Plotinus, *The Enneads, trans* Stephen MacKenna, (1992), Larson Publications

Swami Nikhilananda, tranlator (1963) *The Upanishads*, circa 800 BCE, New York, Humanities Press, Inc. The Upanishads are the discriminative philosophy that emerged from the Vedas about the time that Orphism spread throughout ancient Hellas. The Katha Upanishad is quoted throughout my paper for the verses that are similar to the great Orphic statements and maxims. Indeed, the Orphics referred to one another by the description "Katharoi" or "Pure"— and the Katha is likewise the "Pure" Upanishad.

Karl Jaspers (1957) *Anaximaner, Heraclitus, Parmenids, Plotinus Lao-Tzu Nrgarjuna,* Harcourt Brace, New York

Asklepios, C Kerenyi, 1959

Epidauros, Theodore Papdakins

Appendix: The *Lamella*

#1: (From Petelia: IV-III B.C.) (See Powell, 5th ed., p. 313-316.)

"You will find a spring on the left of the halls of Hades, and beside it a white cypress growing. Do not even go near this spring. And you will find another, from the Lake of Memory, flowing forth with cold water. In front of it are guards. You must say, 'I am the child of Ge and starry Ouranos; this you yourselves also know. I am dry with thirst and am perishing. Come, give me at once cold water flowing forth from the Lake of Memory.' And they themselves will give you to drink from the divine spring, and then thereafter you will reign with the other heroes."

#2: (from Eleutherae in Crete: second century B.C.)

"A: 'I am dry with thirst and am perishing.'

B: 'Come, drink please, from the ever-flowing spring on the right, where the cypress is. Who are you, and where do you come from?'

A: 'I am the son of Earth and Starry Heaven.'"

#3: (from Thurii, in south Italy: (Fourth or third century B.C.)

"A: 'I come from the pure, o Pure Queen of the earthly ones, Eukles, Eubouleus, and You other Immortal Gods! I too claim to be of your blessed race, but Fate and other Immortal Gods conquered me, the star-smiting thunder. And I flew out from the hard and deeply-grievous circle, and stepped onto the crown with my swift feet, and slipped into the bosom of the Mistress (Kore), the Queen of the Underworld. And I stepped out from the crown with my swift feet.'

B: 'Happy and blessed one! You shall be a god instead of a mortal.' A: 'I have fallen as a kid into milk.'"

#4: (from Thurii)

"I come pure from the pure, Queen of the Underworld, Eukles, Eubouleus, and all other gods! For I too claim to be of your race. And I have paid the penalty for unjust deeds, whether Fate conquered me . . . [lacuna] . . . with the thunderbolt and the lightning flash. Now I come as a suppliant to noble Persephone, that she may be kind and send me to the seats of the pure."

#5: (from Rome)

" A: 'I come pure from the pure, Queen of the Underworld, Eukles, Eubouleus, noble child of Zeus! And I have this gift of Memory, prized by men!'
B: 'Caecilia Secundina, come, made divine by the Law!'"

#6: (from Thurii)

"But whenever a soul leaves the light of the sun--enter on the right, where one must, if one has kept all well and truly. Rejoice at the experience! This you have never before experienced. You have become a god instead of a man. You have fallen as a kid into milk. Hail, hail, as you travel on the right, through the Holy Meadow and Groves of Persephone."

#7: (from Thurii)

"To Earth, first-born Mother, Cybelean Kore said: . . . [lacuna] . . .
. . . of Demeter . . . all-seeing Zeus.
O Sun, Fire, you went through all towns, when you appeared with the Victories and Fortunes and All-wise Fate, where you increase the brightness of the festival with your lordship, O glorious deity! By you all things are subdued, all things overpowered, all things smitten! The Decrees of Fate must everywhere be endured. O Fire, lead me to the Mother, if the fast can endure, to fast for seven nights and days! For there was a seven-day fast, O Olympian Zeus and all-seeing Sun . . ."

www.ingramcontent.com/pod-product-compliance
Lightning Source LLC
Chambersburg PA
CBHW031952080426
42735CB00007B/362